HOW TO BE A
PERFECT GRANDMA

BASED ON LOVE AND
SOME CLEVER TRICKS

BY BETTY MARKLE
(AKA) GRANDMA

ISBN-13: 9781492286264
ISBN-10: 1492286265

TABLE OF CONTENTS

1

GAME PLAN

It's every Mother's dream—your daughter is happily married, and she is about to make you a Grandma. Her husband is everything you wished for, and is more of a good friend than a son-in-law. You know they will always be together, and they will make wonderful parents.

Then it hits you, like a frying pan to the head, you are going to be a Grandma. There are few other words that ring out so sweetly. Okay, here it is, right out loud, for the entire world to acknowledge—

"I am going to be a Grandma"

Your delight is overwhelming for; well let's face it, for weeks, before you can calm down enough to make plans. You know, plans on how to be a perfect Grandma.

This could be your only chance to be great at something that really matters. So there can be no errors, at least no major ones.

This child's world will be heavily influenced by everything you do. As for me, well, being a widow, I did not have the help or input of a Grandpa, as I made my plans. It was all up to me. OMG—how could it all have fallen on my shoulders when I had never done this before? But I made myself ready for the challenge.

Remember when you were a child and how you felt about your Grandma? For me, my fondest memories were of my Grandmother. Mary Frances Lancaster was my Mother's mother. She was the sweetest, kindest, most caring woman I had ever known. She had this Grandma thing (or Grandmother-thing, in her case) down to a science. Going to her home was, without a doubt, my favorite thing to do as a child.

I remember how she would open her little change purse and give each grandchild a dime, so we could walk to the corner store for a treat of our choosing. We knew she trusted us with "real cash" and the ability to make a wise decision, all on our own. Wow, how special was that? And then, there was the cherry jello with bananas, in the ice box. You recall what an ice box was, right? Sure you do.

If you are becoming a Grandma, you are very likely a Baby Boomer and your grandparents would have had an ice box, currently referred to as a refrigerator. I can still see the man in his cart bringing the big blocks of ice. But that's another story, and does not help in any way, with the plans at hand.

Point being—Grandmother knew how to make everything perfect. When she made cinnamon toast, it was in the oven, piled with butter and cinnamon sugar. It was not just a slice of toast, it was truly special.

And besides, can you ever remember your favorite grandparent being upset with you? Never happened, even when something went wrong, or was accidently broken. You cried a little and were hugged a lot. The forgiving process usually involved a rocking chair of some kind, kisses, and sweet words of comfort. But you were guaranteed to be fully forgiven, every single time. I just thought it was because Grandmother loved me more than anyone else. Maybe, thinking back now, she was simply a Grandmother with a plan, like you and I.

Let's get started—this little bundle of joy will be here before you know it, and you will want to be ready, in every way.

The following chapters will open your eyes, scare you some, change the world you currently enjoy, and, believe it or not, be the most fun you have ever had.

I raised two daughters who were completely different. Some of my plans worked for both of the girls, but then there were some that simply didn't; and I had to return to the drawing board, as they say, to make adjustments. But I managed, and I made plenty of mistakes, and I continued to adjust the plans, until they were grown. Then I looked back, realized where I could have made better decisions along the way, and understood I did the best I knew how, with the tools at hand, and limited experience. I think all parents reflect back and wish they would have done some things differently. Well, guess what, now we have that chance.

This child will have parents, who will do the hardest part. You and I, well, we get to handle the easy parts. We get to teach, a little; help out, a bit; babysit, some; and hug, a lot. We get to be the sweet, wonderful memory this child will reflect on when grown.

Yup, it's our turn to be magnificent!

One little slip-up and your popularity could start to drop. So, roll up your sleeves, put on a smile, and let's get busy.

2

PARENT'S RULES

It is real—I am a Grandma!!

My little Emma Josephine has arrived and I'm sure I have forgotten something, to begin my well developed, plan. But okay, I will work on it later. Right now—OMG—

I am really a Grandma.

Emma is so sweet she will never know if I make a mistake, and she won't remember later anyway. She doesn't even know I'm her Grandma yet. So, at this point, I need to concentrate on the parent's rules.

My plans include Emma being entrusted to me many times, and I'm sure that it will end abruptly if I don't follow their rules. After all, this is their child, their responsibility, and grandparents are only helpers.

To start, you will want to talk about what Mommy and Daddy expect from Grandma. Listen intently, making mental notes only, so they don't see you writing them down. That would appear lame, and be an indication that you are too old to remember their simple requests.

They may make requests you can't believe. These may actually sound like the same rules you gave to your parents when your first child was born. By the time there was a second child you had stepped into reality, and had given up on the ideal, storybook way of raising a child.

The notion that a child stays beautifully dressed all day, rarely cries at anything milk will not resolve, or never poops beyond the confines of their tiny little diaper, is short lived. New parents, as you will recall, soon discover that their baby, for the most part, is in charge. Dinner schedules, social events, and for sure, sleeping schedules, are all driven by the new little bundle of joy—and so are the rules.

However, it is pretty terrific that the parents are serious about how your grandchild will be raised. They are not taking this new responsibility lightly, and they fully expect you, Grandma, to do your part.

Your daughter, or son, may be thinking they do not want to make all the "errors" you did in your parenting days. Flow with it. They can make their own mistakes along the way. Hopefully they will actually do a better job.

So, now you have their list, or at least their initial list, of the things they expect from you. If you are as lucky as me, the list will be short and simple. Common sense dictates most of it, and the rest are just the desires of the new parents. Don't mess this up Grandma. This is "Test #1" of many. They are watching to see if you can be trusted. You are old, after all, and may have forgotten how to care for a baby.

As silly as that seems, they are somewhat correct. The way we did things was different. Products today are far more advanced, and change how things are done. Doctors have also made new discoveries and found better ideas for child rearing. So even if you think a rule is unnecessary, believe me, it could be valid.

Jump into this new grandparent role with a positive attitude. Use any products you were told to purchase. Follow the routines when asked to babysit this little one. If there is an actual feeding schedule, adhere to it, to the letter. Once you mess up their routine, it is almost impossible to get it back in place; and you, my friend, will have failed "Test #1". So when they need a babysitter next time, they may call someone else. You could miss out on some fun times with your grandchild, not to mention, they will probably wait awhile before moving to "Test #2".

And by the way, rules of the parents are not exclusive to their home alone. They are intended to be followed anywhere their little one is present, including your home.

The parents will be impressed if you make a space in your home specific for your grandchild. It will let them know you want to be wholly involved, and that you are committing time and love to their child. If they only knew just how crazy a Grandma could go with this concept, they would truly be amazed.

Before Emma was born I cleared out the guest room. I sold the furniture and let family members know I would route them to the local hotels for all of their future visits. I then began decorating a nursery for the anticipated visits. Parents will visit more frequently if they do not have to pack a full diaper bag, portable bed for napping, etc. Ah yes, this Grandma provided it all, right down to the diaper cream. Besides, it was a thrill to go shopping and to re-live the days of a baby room. This time however, I did not have to be concerned with the loss of sleep at night. Grandma's little one was bathed, diapered and put into pajamas just prior to the trip back home each time. Such a simple gesture, but totally appreciated by the parents.

As time passes and your little one goes from infancy to the toddler stage you will want to remember to change the room accordingly and childproof your home. This is when you will want to approach the idea of week-end sleep over's. The parents will need to know it is a safe place for their toddler, and that Grandma is on her toes. Let them know the menu, and planned snacks, and make certain you have the same potty arrangements they have at home, so that the training is not interrupted. Let me remind you, this will be a test, no doubt. Think ahead Grandma, plan your activities as well as the meals. Maintain nap and bedtime schedules; bathing your grandchild at the same time they do at home. Make the sleep over's a joy for you, your grandchild, and Mommy and Daddy, who will rediscover grown-up time. My favorite times are the sleep over's because Emma and I have each other exclusively. WOW—what a Grandma rush!

Although my little Emma loved her sleep over's, she began wanting more than the back yard swing set and little pool, inside movies, games, or cookie making. She wanted friends to play with as well. She still desired all of Grandma's attention, but needed more. So, I added some neighbor children; which I already knew, and knew the parents. It gave Emma an extra reason for coming to stay with Grandma, and it helped with entertainment plans. Our evenings were still just the two of us, but it gave her a lot to tell me after the other children left for the day; and our times together became even better.

What about those teen years? Will your plans for a fun week-end need to change? Absolutely! We have to flow with each step as it comes; and recall the fun times wc had when we were that age. Some of the things I remember will probably still be of interest, such as slumber parties, all kinds of food, make-up experimentation, shopping, and discussing boys for hours. The rest will have to fall under the new "parent rules" fit for that age, as that time comes. Grandparents will always need to fall back on the guidelines set by the parents. That's the beauty of being a grandparent. We supply the fun and general good times, while the parents implement the rules.

The Grandma role is the easy one; since we are known for sweetness. We provide great snacks; always have homemade cookies in a special jar, fun meals that are actually healthy, and an abundance of love. No one expects us to ever be harsh, or unfairly judgmental. And, by the way, we have a reputation for always forgiving anything.

One of the "rules" I made at Grandma's house had to be explained to my daughter because it appeared to go against their set of rules. I told Emma, when she was about 2 years old, and experiencing frequent time-out's at home, that there were no time-out's at Grandma's home. Emma gave me no reason to need time-out's at first, believing that was the reason for the rule. However, very shortly, there came the time to test Grandma, and she threw a little fit. Oh, it wasn't much, and I don't recall what it was about anymore. But I looked at her, and said "Emma, you must be kidding". She stopped what she was doing, for a moment, and I promptly sat on the floor facing her. I told her that the reason Grandma never had time-out is because my little "Princess Emma", who, by the way, was seriously into princesses at the time, would never ever act ugly. I told her princesses always acted sweet. She got up from the floor and said "That's a very good idea Grandma" and went back to playing. We still have no time-out at Grandma's, and my daughter understands. Problem resolved, for today.

Emma comes for sleep over's about once a month. Her parents know I will take special care of her, and she will be safe with me. I keep the same medications they use and would always call before giving anything to her. I also have her insurance card in the event of a real emergency, which I will avoid, at all cost. Emma has a complete wardrobe, enough for a week, rotated by size as needed: and I always send her home in a new outfit, since she will wear it more there.

You want your grandchild to feel completely at home at Grandma's. There is no need for a suitcase. She has a built-in home with Grandma.

When Emma comes, her little desk is set up for school time, and her baby is in the stroller ready for a walk when she arrives. She does not need to go find her toys and activities because they are ready for her, just as if she lived with me 24-7. She just walks in, hugs Grandma, and starts playing as if she had never left. Even napping time is relatively easy. When it's time to rest, since she no longer takes scheduled structured naps, she will go to her shelf, select one of her movies to share with Grandma, and crawl up beside me on the couch or recliner. Very shortly she slips off to sleep, and I slip into heavenly bliss.

I still maintain the schedules she has at home, and she knows I will, so there is no struggle. Seven o'clock at home is bath time and eight o'clock is bedtime. I have adhered to those rules since day-one, and when I announce that it is seven o'clock, she stops whatever she is doing and heads for the bath. It is just as easy at eight o'clock. As soon as I tell her what time it is, she goes to the story book bin and selects two stories. She climbs in my lap, in my rocker, as has always been our tradition, for our reading time. Then she goes straight to her bed for nightly prayers, a kiss and off to sleep.

While your grandchild is small the rules are pretty easy and most children become accustomed to a routine fairly quickly, as long as it stays consistent. It is a matter-of-fact situation and works well.

Be flexible, parent rules change as parents discover new ways of doing things, or as they realize some of the original rules are no longer necessary. In some cases, depending on the child, the rules will be relaxed due to the way the child is developing. Whatever you do, never criticize the rules. Remember, this is not your child, and not your responsibility, as far as the big picture is concerned. You are a relative. Yes, you understood me correctly, I said "relative". It may sound distant, but it is still the truth. You have to earn your place of importance, and being a cooperative relative, a "rule-following", always agreeable relative, will get you to the place you want to be. You will become the Grandma they speak fondly of to their friends. You will be the one they can count on, and your grandchild will delight with the idea of being with you.

Now, let's address a rule that most parents insist we all follow, and it is probably one of the most difficult. You have been told, along with the rest of the family, that you are restricted as to the number of gifts you can buy this sweet child. How can this be? Oh, their reasoning is sound, as they realize they need to maintain the number of toys in their child's world. They also want to prevent spoiling, or favoritism, driven by volumes of toys. They are right, naturally, but it is a rule that requires real will power.

You walk into the largest toy establishment in the city, in search of the perfect birthday present. You are met by every toy imaginable and you know how much your grandchild would love each one. So, if you settle on a doll, is it acceptable to include a bed, stroller, high chair, bottle and clothes? Not likely. It requires practice, it takes control, and real determination to enter a toy store and walk out with a single gift. And what about the gift; should it be educational, which would please Mommy and Daddy; or, should it simply be something to thrill your grandchild? I vote for the grandchild, so you get to experience the delight as the gift is opened and a hug for your selection.

You can always ask permission to buy clothes. With the rules I am following, you can add all the clothes you want as long as you only buy one single toy. The clothes help the parents, and the child has more packages to unwrap, although the delight is limited. Fortunately, Emma is thrilled by pretty little dresses, and I get to fulfill my shopping desires without guilt. You can also ask about monetary gifts toward their education. I cannot imagine being denied that offer, and it feels good to a Grandma.

So, you see, there are ways to follow rules that leave room for flexibility. Talk to the parents. After all, they are the ones planning your grand-child's future. Let them know how much you want to help. Remember, they are still the PARENTS—

And you—you are the GRANDMA—working on perfection!

3

TEACHING YOUR GRANDCHILD

Remember when you were young and patience was difficult to maintain? Guess what, it is easier now, believe it or not, you will find you have endless patience with your grandchild as they try to learn something new. You will find yourself watching closely as each step begins as a struggle and then falls into place. You will feel the delight of success right along with this child, and be ready for the next challenge.

Perhaps it is because you know you are not in charge of their training. You have the freedom to fail and their parents will pick up where you left off. You, on the other hand, will be given credit for introducing something new, and getting the ball rolling.

Everything you can think of to teach your little one can begin with a game, making it immediately interesting. I often put what I would like her to memorize, to music. If a child can learn their ABC's in a song, they can learn anything.

I recently had Emma for a four day sleep over and taught her a song about family.

> D-A-D-D-Y spells Daddy,
> M-O-M-M-Y spells Mommy,
> E-M-M-A spells Emma,
> And we are family.

Not only did I add music, but gestures as well, just as there are gestures for "I'm a Little Teapot". She picked it up quickly and we sang it off and on throughout the four days. She was thrilled to share her song when she arrived back home. She can now spell all three names.

Playing school is a favorite activity at Grandma's, nearly every time she comes. She will pick the dolls and stuffed animals she wants to use as other classmates; and takes quite a while arranging them in just the right order. She always places herself in the center seat and Grandma becomes the teacher. Lessons will be short while your grandchild is young; and praise is extremely important. As I see the interest fading away, I move to "arts and crafts" or "music time". If I am completely losing her, I will call for "gymnastics"; that almost always works. We can then go to snack time and school is dismissed. School for ages 2-3 years is likely to be a whopping 20-30 minutes. As they get older, and you get better ideas, the lessons can stretch out longer.

On occasion, one of the "stuffed" students must be corrected, and told to be quiet, or told to stop playing with their toes, or counting monkeys in class. The more creative reason you use to interrupt the class, the more fun it becomes for your favorite student. And remember, you need a silly teacher's voice, not your own. You can even dress funny. Laughter creates a winning atmosphere.

Then there is the game of teaching a dolly how not to pick up things that can break. Your grandchild will become the teacher and can explain why items on the coffee table, dressers, what-not displays, etc. cannot be handled. They will learn by teaching someone else, and you, Grandma, can emphasize how smart they are for teaching their babies how to treat items that are not toys.

Follow that exercise by letting them show their babies where the toys are kept, so they can explain that those are the items meant to be picked up, and played with. Then, stop what you are doing, and play.

Cooking lessons, on the other hand, need special attention. When Emma was about 18 months old I placed one of the little children's kitchens in my kitchen, so we could cook at the same time. I provided a drawer full of plastics, just for her use, and a shopping cart full of food. The minute I headed for the kitchen, she would follow, put on her little cooking mitt, which was hung by Velcro on the end of the cabinet, and begin cooking.

Kitchens can be a dangerous place for our grandchildren and we had to establish some rules right away. If Grandma was going to open the oven door, Emma had to open her oven door, across the room, at the same time. Children love to mimic so it can be easier than you would imagine keeping them from a hot oven. Thinking, on your part, will keep sharp instruments in the sink in lieu of on the counter, and pots on the back burners only. And if you think cooking is only for little girls you would be wrong. Little boys like being creative in the kitchen as well.

So here you are, as they get old enough to begin actually helping. They will want to sift the flour, crack the eggs, add milk and oil and—OMG--mix it. This could begin at 2 to 3 years of age, and since they do not have perfect control of their cooking skills at that age, you are guaranteed to experience a real mess, possibly a disaster, in your nice clean kitchen. Enjoy the thrill of your grandchild learning something new, while they concentrate on their efforts, knowing Grandma will not be upset if a mess is the end result. Make certain that whatever is being created is actually cooked, and eaten.

Grandma's house should always be a fun place, and your reaction to their efforts must always be positive. The experience, after they have gone home, and you reflect back on it, should make you smile, or even laugh. After all, it should make you proud that there was a bonding time between you, and no hurt feelings. Did it taste bad? Fake it Grandma. No matter what, there must be praise.

You have now found other children in the neighborhood the right age to be playmates, and you are already comfortable with the parents, and the children, and your plan is to invite them over when your grandchild comes next time.

Emma was thrilled to go to their home, meet their Mommy, and the girls that she was inviting over to play later that day. We talked about how important it is to have friends, and to be ready to share our toys. She was ready and anxious when they arrived. It was a beautiful spring day and Emma was 3 years old. The girls, who are well behaved, bonded easily; and I'm proud to say that Emma shared her toys and her swing set wonderfully.

What I did not expect, was that she was unwilling to share her Grandma, at all. Anytime I assisted, or spoke kindly with one of the other girls, Emma ran to me and immediately wanted to be held. I held her, but still worked with the other children. Little by little I realized I could maintain eye contact, and a smile, with Emma, as I pushed another on the swing, or marveled at something they showed me. As time went on, my attention was less necessary, and playing with her new friends took priority. Emma realized I was still going to be her Grandma, even when others came to play. After they left we spent special time talking about the fun we had, and how proud I was of her.

Jealousy can be hurtful to a child and can cause them to be ugly to those stealing the attention they are unwilling to share. By showing Emma she was still my special one, and not pushing her away, she naturally felt the love we shared was still there, and she could be comfortable to enjoy her friends. The praise that followed, and the reminder that she was my little love, took care of future fears as well.

Reinforcing love cannot be done too often. Rest assured there will be those who will accuse you of spoiling your grandchild. Let me explain the word "spoiling". When something is spoiled it has gone bad. To spoil something you would be making it worse that it was before; it is a negative result to an effort. You are spoiling a child when you replace love and interest, and caring, and time spent, with material possessions. If you are of the mind-set that you can buy the love of a child with the purchase of toys, you are wrong. Love from a child is earned, and developed by the love you give. Memories of Grandma, that will last a lifetime, are those of time spent together and the laughter shared. They will recall the times they broke something, or spilled something, and your reaction. They will remember you were understanding and kind. They will also remember the lack of anger throughout their childhood. And isn't that our goal? We each want to be the kind of Grandma our grandchildren cling to, tell everything to, and trust. We want to be the memory that is warm and loving. Well guess what, you are the only one who can create that memory. Bad experiences, angry words, disappointing glances, and ugly reactions to a child simply trying to be a child, will last forever. An apology after the fact will not erase a hurtful experience, and the memory is now in place.

Now, let's talk about your family pet, perhaps an older pet, not used to children. After all, your children have been gone a long time. This is a challenge for you, as well as for "Fido". We'll just use Fido as our generic name to make our conversation flow easier. Fido is more interesting than any toy you could possibly offer, as your grandchild becomes a toddler. This is the only toy with genuine reactions to them. Unfortunately, Fido cannot understand your warning about toddlers, and your toddler is in the same situation.

You will need to monitor their time together and stay involved. If Fido is an indoor/outdoor pet you can separate them easily and only put them together for short play periods under close supervision, as you teach them how to interact. On the other hand, if Fido is an indoor pet only, you will need to put him up during the times you are not working on training, just as you do when guests come over who are allergic to animals, or are elderly.

You will want to provide Fido with additional attention when your toddler is down for a nap. And, by all means, let them spend as much time together, supervised, as you can, so they become accustomed to each other. As the toddler stage makes way to a 4-5 year old child, the bond needs to already be well established. They will be best friends, and your home will be a special place to visit.

Remember, training is easier without scolding. There is no place in the process for upset feelings or tears; make it a fun, learning experience. If you see that Fido shows a negative reaction, just explain that he is learning how to play, and explain why he reacted as he did. Tell your toddler we will let him rest for now. Then, before putting them together again, do a reminder on what upset Fido last time, so it can be avoided this time.

Let's move on now to manners. There are table manners, or being polite when we introduce them to our friends at church or in the neighborhood, or even if we take them to the grocery store. It can make a Grandma beam if our little ones are sweet when introduced to someone. It's easy when they are infants, everyone delights at a baby. It's the toddler stage I'm talking about, and beyond. I guarantee your toddler will try to use tactics they saw at daycare to get everything they can, the first time you take them shopping. But remember, we are older, and wiser than they can even imagine. So when you gently reject the "I wants" until they become demands, in hopes that their loving Grandma will give in; you will require excellent skills. You certainly do not need a screaming child embarrassing you; or a crying child believing you are failing as the perfect Grandma, just because they do not grasp your rejection to their wants. Stop what you are doing, look sweetly at your toddler and tell them how much you love them, and how sad you are that they do not feel well."It's okay Honey; Grandma can take us back home so you are not so unhappy". Then give them a sweet hug and head for the check-out. Explain you were going to get those special ice cream bars you know they liked, but since they feel bad, you will have to get them next time. I promise you they will not want to miss out on the ice cream, and will re-think their actions. They will announce they feel much better now. You need to react positively by telling them how happy it makes you, because it was hurting your feelings when they were so upset. That usually completes this one trip, but you will want to set a pattern. So next time you go to the store, be sure and tell them you are planning to get their favorite "whatever" and make sure it is the final item on your list. You are always free to pick up something extra as you praise their perfect behavior, but don't go overboard. Make good manners an expected behavior.

Too often we expect small children to use "Yes Sir" as they speak to strangers we introduce them to at church. I know it's cute, but let's remember it is also unnecessary. Do not make a production of wording. Let a toddler be polite in their own words. If it becomes a rehearsed introduction, they may simply not speak, out of fear of a mistake. And then there is the church social. Heaven forbid you should be embarrassed by bad table manners. Please remember that absolutely everyone realizes you are not the training parent, you are Grandma, and at the mercy of how the parents are teaching this child. I am lucky enough that little Emma is taught really well at home.

You can do your part as you emphasize how thrilled you are every time they use their fork or spoon instead of their fingers. Show them how to use a napkin, like a "grown-up"; that's something everyone finds cute. Whatever manners you can teach will be used in front of your friends, simply because toddlers are natural show-offs. If they think it's funny to play in their food, they will. But, if you delight when the use a spoon, or a napkin, that's what they will do instead.

Your part, in the training process, although only a part-time influence in their over-all development, is critical to the times they spend with you. Believe it or not, it will infiltrate into their home life. Emma loves to show the new things she has learned with Grandma, when she goes home. And, although her Mommy and Daddy need no help with her training, they enjoy her delight showing off, and appreciate what I share with Emma.

Yes indeed, these are each bonding times, and experiences to be remembered.

4

GIVING UP ON A CLEAN HOME

You've raised your family, and the days of socks under the bed, toys on the floor in every room, and a general mess on every counter top, are over. You can actually sit on the couch without having to move notebooks, sweaters, or a variety of other unnecessary items. Your home stays "company ready" most of the time. Everything is in its place, decorations are nicely displayed, all beds are made, and throw pillows are everywhere you want them. There are no empty chip bags throughout the house, upsetting your scheme; and you love your home again, just as you did before you started raising a family. Now please, don't misunderstand me, you, I'm sure, loved the years of rearing children as much as I did. There were no regrets when you dealt with the mess in your "house", as it became a "home". The joy of raising children and developing young adults is probably one of the most rewarding things anyone can experience. We, as parents, would never change that part of our lives.

But now, we are the famous empty-nesters, retired, or nearly retired citizens, bragging on how well we did as parents, or at least how well we tried. We reflect on our own mistakes along the way, and are grateful how well our children turned out in spite of our errors. So, here we are, embarking on our next adventure. We are grandmas and have new opportunities ahead of us, as we plan how everything will be. Some of us set up a nursery in preparation of playtime at Grandma's. We are anticipating all the good times ahead from infancy through college and possibly marriage. We are going to be perfect. There will be no room for errors. After all, we raised our children and know the pit-falls already. Besides, anything new coming along will be handled by our children, the parents of this sweet baby. So we can relax this time and be the "icing" on the "cake of life", and the perfect part of this child's world.

The nursery will be just right, and will be spotless. Spit-ups will be handled immediately, as will diapers. After all, the house is clean, and the only thing that will require attention is this one small room. It can't get any easier. And that's true for awhile, until the nursery becomes a toddler's room. You will want to provide real toys like building blocks, stuffed animals of all sizes, puzzles, books, games, etc. A toy box is a good idea because you believe you will immediately train your toddler to put everything away before getting something new out. Hurrah for you; you will be the first Grandma in history to make that happen, and still be popular. The last thing on a toddler's mind is maintaining your tidy home. They want to play with everything at the same time, and they want to play with you as well. All stuffed animals will want to be in the living room together, so no one feels left out. Certainly you can understand that, right Grandma? And, they might get cold, so we need blankets, or towels, for each one. Not to mention, they will each want a story book to read. Depending on the number of animals you purchased, because they were too cute to resist, your living room could take on a really crowded appearance. Now you might think to yourself, this isn't too bad, it's just one room at a time, and you can handle that. But that's not how it works. Interest is short lived, and they move on to the kitchen, where they find all the wonderful plastics you have provided, which all need to be on the floor at the same time. It's a cute scene for sure, and in your mind, you think you can clean up the living room while you toddler is entertained by the plastics in the kitchen. No, you don't dare leave them unattended, you know that. You need to stay and supervise; and besides, your presence is requested. It wouldn't have worked anyway because if you had started putting the animals away they would have come right back out.

Their room is also turned upside down by now and all the building blocks are on the floor, along with every other toy available. Toddlers move from room to room with a delight and level of energy we have forgotten. You will introduce gates at an early age just to maintain some of your sanity, and control, as training is implemented. Believe me when I tell you, that bedrooms, if they have access to them, are a true joy. Bedrooms have beds, and if your toddler is too short to climb on the beds on their own, they will surely get their little step stool, so they can reach their intended goal, and bounce wildly. What step stool? Well, that would be the one you provided beside the grown-up potty, so little people can get to their own little potty seat. You know the same little stool they use to wash their hands and splash water on the once spotless mirrors. In time it may be the same step stool they use to climb on the counters, unless you pay attention to what I am writing.

Back to the bedroom—there are dresser drawers, some easy enough to open. I feel relatively certain you have not added childproof latches to your drawers, which make them fair game.

But you see, some of this can easily be avoided, if you are a perfect Grandma. The whole concept of being perfect is based on how you are perceived by your grandchild. And what they want more than toys, or bouncing on beds, is you, and your undivided attention. You are the sweet, wonderful playmate who will never hit or kick or become angry. You, Grandma will let them win at every game and marvel at anything they do. You never notice mistakes, but you are ready to assist when needed.

When Emma and I fill the living room with stuffed animals and play whatever game she thinks of, I steer her in the direction I want. I may, at some point, ring the school bell so everyone can find their seat for class. Make it a brief one, ring the bell again for recess so everyone can dance around, then ring it again for dismissal and everyone can march home to the toy box. Living room clean-up is now complete.

Now on to the kitchen, quickly, before you lose your window of opportunity. Sort the plastics by colors, or sizes, making a game of it, possibly with a prize to be won. Play along to see who can stack more bowls first. Then tear them down for the next game. If your little one realizes you are only cleaning up it will end quickly. Once interest begins to fade it becomes reward time, such as taking only a yellow bowl and a plastic spoon and painting it with ice cream; or using a pop-cycle to paint it, eating as you go. Then send your toddler to get the step stool so they can share in washing dishes, just like a real restaurant owner. It can also be fun to let them make a menu once they know what is being served for lunch, and let them set the table. Surely you can eat a meal served on plastic dishes once in a while. Be flexible; add silly items to the menu like one green elephant, or six upside-down monkeys. Children love to be funny; and they will delight in Grandma being funny as well.

The kitchen is clean, lunch has been served, and you are free to head to the playroom for some real play time.

When weather permits, the best way to keep your home in order is to stay outside. Outside toys are easy to supply, such as a good soccer ball for endless kicking. They love to kick, chase after the ball, and kick it back, over and over. This activity requires very little participation from you, in the event you are getting tired. If you have purchased a swing set, that can entertain them for hours, as long as you are willing to push the swings and delight in their happiness every time they go down the slide. Use the garden hose in hot weather to spray them or fill their pools. But maintain constant supervision Grandma; our grandchildren count on us for their safety. Do not turn your back for a moment. Always have a towel ready so you do not carry half of the yard back into the house when it's time to go in.

For the first few years there is that wonderful period of time known as nap-time. Take full advantage and clean up whatever you can while they sleep ever so sweetly. It doesn't take long, without their help, and you will still have time for a satisfying cup of coffee in the silence. Cherish the moment, because following nap-time is pure energy. Be prepared to play, because you are "the best", as my Emma calls me, when we are playing together.

By the simple nature of having a child in your home you will be left with gifts, after they have gone. Every mirror that was within reach will have hand prints. Every glass topped table will be covered with tiny fingers, as well as glass doors, curio cabinet fronts, etc. And yes, even the black refrigerator, dishwasher, and oven doors will display the markings of small hands. You may find yourself not cleaning them off right away. It makes you feel as if they are still with you. I have been known to wait a week, or longer, before removing such wonderful reminders of a visit. My home will be well cleaned except for a variety of handprints.

You will want to pat yourself on the back at this point, realizing that you are becoming an expert at keeping your home relatively tidy, while maintaining your popularity. That, however, only covers the big picture, there could be spills that would stain the furniture, or food ground into the rugs or carpet. The best way to control that problem is to contain all eating to the kitchen and breakfast area. Good luck with that.

Meals are easy because they are traditionally served at the table. Snacks are another issue. One trick is to design what their snacks will be. For example, the drink offered will have a specific type of cup. In my home Emma has a cup for water that is a thermos. She likes to hear the ice against the sides, and it has its own, attached straw, and a flip lid which closes it completely. That one can be taken to the living room when watching a movie. Juice has a different cup, one that was selected by her and is used specifically for juice. It lives only in the kitchen, right along with the special cup she uses for milk. There is no request to carry the open topped cups to any other room, because it simply isn't an option. So the issue of spills on the furniture or carpet is not a problem. Spills are in the kitchen, and tile is a simple clean up. Serve small amounts in the cups, more often, rather than a large amount at one time, that also helps prevent accidents.

Sticky snacks such as fruit are always at the kitchen table, and Grandma participates. Cheese sticks, which seem to require being pulled apart, can be messy and must also be eaten at the table. The only types of snack I allow her to eat from a cup in her lap are things that are clean, such as gold fish crackers. They can be eaten whole and are clean. Some of the dried fruit chips work as well. Emma's favorite snack is yogurt and that is definitely a table treat. You can always ask your grandchild what kind of snack they want, and even make a chart which will show them which snacks are kitchen snacks, and which can be eaten from their lap. The chart becomes a rule, so do not take blame if you cannot allow a snack to be taken to the living room when the chart indicates "kitchen". The rules are the rules" after all.

As your grandchild gets older they will probably find your rules to be silly, but guess what, they will still be used as the rules of Grandma's house; and if you keep them in place, while their age requires them, they will still accept them, no matter how silly. It is a matter of consistency, this is the way you have always had your home, and you have always been kind and loving about it. That's the part that will stay with them, not the rules that they became accustomed to over the years. It will be your sweetness toward them they will remember. Revel in your success knowing they will one day look back at how wonderful the times were at Grandma's house. I remember how happy it made my Grandmother when I put things away, or cleaned up from a snack. I loved showing her what I had done, just for her, just because I loved her. I knew how happy it made her, and me.

Be sure, over the years, to praise their efforts. Thank them for cleaning up all of their toys, although you can see the entire stack pushed and piled under the play table. The rest of the room may be spotless as a result, and your sweet grand-child will be incredibly proud of a job well done. Be delighted, give a big hug and suggest the toys would be happier in the toy box. By all means, help move them at this point.

Welcome to your successful plan for keeping a fairly clean home while holding on to your perfect Grandma status.

5

HOW TO SAY "NO" SUCCESSFULLY

Pay attention Grandma, this is going to be a real challenge. There will be times when you have to decline something your grandchild wants, or wants to do. It is a careful balancing act to maintain that perfect status, and use the "No" word. The trick is to replace it with other words that work equally as well. It will be tempting as your grandchild enters the "testing" years. What do they call them? Oh yes, terrible twos and traumatic threes. But hang on, remember you are wise and experienced. Surely you can slip right past those stages and sail on to smoother waters, without a snag.

I can recall Emma's first little "fit" in my hallway. I don't even remember what it was she wanted to do anymore, but I remember telling her we could do it after dinner. She threw herself on the carpet and began her little fit. Initially it was a surprise, and then I chuckled at her and said "Really?", and walked past her. She promptly got up and followed me to the kitchen where I was headed to begin dinner. I pretended it had never taken place and asked if she wanted to help cook. She said "yes" and we went on about our business. The next day I had asked her, during play time, if she needed to "potty" and she hollered very loudly, "no". I looked at her and said, "Oh, my goodness, I guess you forgot Grandma could hear you just fine in a little girl voice". She responded that she didn't need to go potty, and I, being wise, stated that it was okay. I told her I believed her, because a pretty little princess would not wet her panties. She looked up at me and calmly announced she was going to the potty, which she did. I responded as if it was new news. I did not address the loud voice she had previously used because I didn't need to. It has not happened again.

Children develop by trying new things, testing their limits I suppose. All of this is fine, and normal, but needs to be guided in the right direction. It is up to their teachers, parents, and yes, grandparents, to teach them how to use these new found feelings. Emma was playing "Doctor" not long ago and was checking my ears for monkeys, as he doctor does with her, when she said there were none, because Grandma can hear really well when Emma talks in a princess voice. I was elated because I realized she had correctly registered what I told her over a year ago. They will surprise you at how easily they learn, and their level of retention.

When your grandchild starts to do something unsafe, your immediate reaction word is usually "No". Practice using other options such as "I don't think so" or "that won't work" or even "that's far too dangerous". Remove the child from the situation, while using your new phrases, and follow it with an explanation so they understand your concern.

You could even use a favorite cartoon hero if you prefer, such as, Buz would never climb on the table and jump off, because it is not safe". We believe Buz, don't we? The key is that the word "No" normally comes without a reason. We never want our grandchildren hurt, and we want them to know it.

Sometimes the refusal is not related to danger at all. It can be because we are just too tired to do what they want; and what they are asking requires a great deal of physical involvement on our part. Try the truth. Tell your energetic toddler you are tired, but that you have a great idea. Be prepared to offer something they will enjoy, and that requires more observing than participating. Make sure the new idea requires their imagination and creativity so it holds their interest. You remember the old joke about the parent who purchased an expensive toy for their child that did absolutely everything? The child was soon bored and began playing with the box, where he could be creative. You would be surprised how much fun a large box can be if you provide crayons and let them do whatever they want.

Moving on, there is the refusal to buy something they have their eye on at the store. Everything they see can be an "I want that, Grandma", or the very polite "May I please have that Grandma?" It is easier to deny them a toy when they do not end their request with that sweet word "Grandma". You heard me, it makes it personal. The desire for something is directed only to you, the one person who could never say "No". You realize you can't always agree with everything they want; it would absolutely send the wrong message. That is not what Grandma is all about. Grandma is for fun, and hugs, and always being ready to listen and understand; you are not intended to be the year-round Santa Clause. Don't save your shopping chores for when you have your grandchild with you. Plan to have your shopping already completed in advance and only shop when the intent is to make a purchase for your little one.

Let it be known what the trip is for, such as a new wading pool, and buy only that. If you planned to include pool toys then tell them there will be three toys, and allow them to make the selections.

I had a recent experience when I went with my daughter to one of the local stores, and I had promised Emma a small stuffed toy as a treat for being so good all day, since I knew she had not been feeling her best. She selected one, but then another caught her eye. I suggested she hold each one so she could change her mind, if she wanted. She was allowed to make her own decision, which she did, and we put the first one back. It went so well that we went through the same process several more times, until she had exactly what she wanted. I praised her for taking the time to pick very carefully so she would be able to keep the very best one. She took pride in the fact she had made her own decision. And I did not have to face the "I want them both" dilemma. Even the smallest child wants to be trusted so you will know how smart they are. They are hungry for new challenges, be ready to offer the opportunities.

Next you will face the "I don't want to" or "I can't do that". It is really the same thing. Look at what you are asking them to do, and ask yourself why they don't want to. Very likely it is simply because of timing. Are they in the middle of a play time where they are being creative already? Are they building something, creating with clay, or acting out a story with different characters? These are the activities you do not want to interrupt. These are the important development times you want to encourage. Whatever you are asking of them may not be a good idea at this time, and is it necessary? Perhaps what you want them to do is something they failed at previously, and they are afraid of failing again. Ask them why they do not want to do what you are requesting. Insist on a real answer, listen, and remember this is from the heart of a small child. If they truly believe they will fail, or get scolded for not doing it correctly, provide reassurance. Let them know you will do it together.

My Emma was becoming very skilled at simple puzzles so I began buying more advanced ones. Unfortunately, on a day when she was already tired, she became frustrated and brushed the pieces from the table to the floor, and became upset. This could have resulted in a spoiled day, but not with Grandma. We just gathered the pieces and decided to do something else. I assured her we would do it another time, together, and it would be okay. I offered her one of her movies; she sat in my lap and fell asleep within about 10 minutes. She just needed a nap, although she believes she can go all day without one. With nap time over, the movie turned off, and a small snack together, we pulled out the puzzle. I told her I would need her help. Each time I put a couple of pieces together, she would say "Good job Grandma" and we would "high 5". I did the same with her, and soon the simple "high 5's" became squeals of delight as we watched the picture develop. Before long it was completed, and there was plenty of praise for a job well done. When she woke the next morning she was ready for the challenge of another puzzle. They must believe they can do anything you ask of them, because Grandma would never ask anything they couldn't do. Build their confidence so they are ready to take on the next project. They will thrive on the anticipation of what is in store for them, and Grandma's house will become a place of adventure. The knowledge that you will not let them fail will give them the desire to try harder. And let me tell you, just knowing they will not be scolded for making a mistake, is even more important.

Set the stage early so your grandchild will understand how to "be" at Grandma's house. Love is abundant, and Grandma is patient. They will be allowed to touch some things, but will need to ask if it okay to touch others. At first, Emma would go from decoration to decoration, wanting to pick up and hold everything. I took the time to show her everything and even tell her who everyone was in each photo. Then I explained that kissing her fingers and touching everyone was better than picking up the pictures. I explained that the table decorations were pretty to look at but weren't any fun to hold because they were not a game. I said, "oh well, they are just pretty to look at", which satisfied her. Each time, while she was small, we would begin our visits with the same routine, so we could go on to other things.

Then there are those decorations intended to be handled, ever so gently. I have a small window next to the front door where I place seasonal decorations that are not breakable. She understood that whatever was in that window was okay to pick up, and even carry around. I pretended it they were special, but that Grandma trusted Emma to take very good care of them. She would leave all of the other decorations alone and go straight for that window. She would bring whatever was there, over to me, and announce that she was being very careful. She would hold the item for a bit, and then return it to the window. She was obviously proud of the fact that I would trust her to take care of something that was special to me. It gave her pride.

There are more reasons than I can count for using the dreaded "No" word, but even more great ways to avoid it. One of my favorite experiences with Emma was when she used the "No" response, on Grandma, during bath time. I have a garden tub in the master bathroom which is where Emma takes her bathes when she stays over. We fill it with bubbles and plenty of tub toys. Once actual bathing has been completed, I allow her to play and entertain Grandma with her games. She would probably stay in the tub for hours if I let her, but at some point it is time to get out, and into pajamas. I had to work and work at convincing her it was the end of bath time, but she always wanted a few more minutes. Then I realized that if I pulled the plug while she was playing, the water would empty out, and she would become chilly. It was at that point she was anxious to leave the tub and accept the warm towel Grandma was holding. Problem resolved.

Let's face it---"No" is negative, and your grandchild expects only positive responses from you. Think before you speak, recall the clever tricks you learned from raising you own children, and replace the negative reactions with positive actions---and a hug.

6

LISTEN TO YOUR
GRANDCHILD

One of the greatest advantages grandmas have over parents is time. Normally you are already retired and no one dictates your schedule. You are not pressured to buy groceries, clean house, plan meals, garden, do laundry, and on and on, while spending most of your day at work. My goodness, how did you ever manage it all, and raise your children? Well, who knows, you just did. Unfortunately, you were unable to spend as much quality time as you wanted, listening to your children. Just ask them today and they will agree.

But now, that hectic life is behind you; not only are you not rushing off to work, but you aren't raising a family either. It's all done and in the wonderful past. You are ready to embark on being the kind of grandma you can take pride in knowing is, well, perfect. The one thing you know to be crucial to a child is for someone to listen to what they have to say. They will not have to call your name five or six times before being acknowledged. Even if you are in the middle of a conversation with someone else, when you hear a soft sweet voice call your name, you turn and listen. That's what perfect Grandma's do.

You will want to excuse yourself from your current conversation and pay attention, full attention to this small child's need. Look directly at them so they know you are interested in what they have to say, and respond in kind words, no matter how silly the conversation really is. Remember a child's vocabulary, level of experience, and practice with communication, is limited to only a few years of sheltered life.

Your Grandma status will climb by leaps and bounds if you are an intent listener. Don't become bored and cut them off, listening is far more important than most anything else you could be doing. And guess what, as your little one gets older, they will still come to you when they want to talk, and be heard. Too often as the pre-teen years make their way into teen difficulties, they discover it is hard to find someone to confide in who will not judge them, and who will truly listen to their concerns. That will be you Grandma. The toddler warmth will grow into teen trust, for the one who loves them beyond measure. You will set the pace right now, just by being patient and attentive. Besides, it can be fun to hear what they find interesting. The things we find important, like money issues, health topics, politics, and what the neighbors are doing wrong, are of no interest to our grandchild. It is far more important to make sure the green frog is seated beside the pink bunny, when tea is served.

Many of their conversations require your participation as someone other than who you are. I have been known to be several different story book characters, dogs, cats, and anything else Emma could create in her imagination. But if the current conversation becomes too silly to handle, you can always steer it in another direction. That's one of the wonderful things about children, they can move from one topic to another without a problem, or even to an activity. Just be very careful, you do not want your grandchild to think you are bored, or tired of listening to them. That would be a negative reaction that you would not want to relay.

One afternoon, when Emma was tired, due to the lack of a nap, and a very busy day of outside play, and her conversation was lacking in topic, I knew I had to make a change. I suggested we allow her animals to join us. She could tell each one a different story, and I would be their voice back to her. It gave the conversation some direction; and once we had gone through the grown-up animals, we were done. She crawled in my lap, told me I was "the best", and as I rocked her, she fell asleep. The experience was positive for her, entertaining for me, and managed to work into a nap that she was certain she didn't need. As I watched her rest in my lap I knew she had been satisfied with the conversation we shared. Many of our talks still have limited structure, but they are important.

There have been times when I initiated a conversation as a tool to get away from a difficult situation. Children, like the rest of us, can become frustrated when what they are doing is not going well, especially if they are tired, or perhaps not feeling their best at the time. Instead of pointing out how upset your grandchild is, and trying to sooth the situation, suggest we tell a story. Invite them to tell a "pretend" story about their stuffed frog having tea with the bunny. You can always provide the beginning and they will, I guarantee, pick it up from there. "Froggy is silly when he dribbles tea on his tummy, isn't he?" Okay, now you have the start of a real conversation, and the end of an upsetting situation. Pretend to giggle now and then, and you are on a roll Grandma. Then speak with the frog and bunny so they can join the story. From there you can move into a game you create with the four of you. Always remember that the intent of all of this is to see happiness in your little one. Emma and I were in the middle of a similar situation one day, and as we entered the "game" stage she looked at me and told me I was her best friend. Let me tell you that it will warm you all over, because when it comes unsolicited from a small child it is genuine. It is how they truly feel about you, at that very moment. I scooped her up and gave her a Grandma hug, telling her how much I loved her. I will never forget that day.

Let me now warn you, about you. That's right; so far we have discussed your grandchild's irritations, and how to react as a grandma. You have willingly agreed to have your sweet, wonderful grandchild next Friday. You make plans for activities and are looking forward to the fun the two of you will share. Then Friday comes, and you feel bad, perhaps it was the way you slept the night before, who knows, but your headache is worse than ever. You have already taken all you can, medically, but the headache is still there. No, it isn't bad enough to cancel your plans, but you need to be really careful. Normal toddler reactions to the day's activities or usually seen as cute, or can at least be re-directed. Today however, they may actually get on your nerves, or irritate you enough that you react negatively. Careful Grandma, what you say and do will remain in this precious child's heart. You do not want ugly words taken as a sign that "Grandma doesn't love me anymore". Once a bad reaction is received by a child, it will last, sometimes into their adult life.

My Grandma Maude Ella, my father's mother, once told me she wished her son had never been born. She was apparently very angry with him at the time and did not think about the age of her audience. I asked her what would happen then. "You wouldn't have me if Daddy hadn't been born"; and her return comment absolutely broke my heart. She announced that "that would be okay". I have never forgotten that day, and I was probably only 6 or 7 years old. I can still recall the nights I cried, truly believing she didn't love me. I didn't realize that it was only anger against my father, or that she was just in a terrible mood. Grandma didn't love me, and that was the only thing that registered.

Her visits no longer made me happy although she would tell me she loved me, because I knew better. For a long time her visits were hurtful; and then they no longer mattered at all. On the other hand, my Grandmother, on my mother's side, never spoke unkind to me. I knew, always, that she loved me without measure.

Now that I'm grown I can fully understand what really happened that day so long ago. But guess what, it still hurts a bit, as silly as that may seem. I cannot recall the good times we had before that day, but there must have been many. The only thing that remains, when I remember Grandma, is hurt.

So when you are angry, or just not generally feeling your best, be very careful. There is a child intently listening to your every word. I believe that sometimes adults forget the importance of our words or actions, on children. They love us, and have since the first time we held them close. Do not, for any selfish, misguided reason, damage that love. Cancel your visit if you are not certain you can be the warm wonderful Grandma you need to be.

So, you have this still lingering headache, but you feel confident you can control any negative display with your grandchild. You have been look-ing forward to this day and really want to enjoy it. Well then, let's incorporate your headache into your day's activities. Surely any grandchild has a "Doctor's kit". Tell them Grandma has a headache and needs a Doctor. Believe me, they will be more than happy to take care of you, and you can lie back on the couch while they do. Continue the day with simple activities where your grandchild is the active participant and you are doing mostly observing.

If you feel yourself slipping, possibly getting a little frustrated at what would not normally bother you, stop and re-group. Tell your little one how happy you are they came to play, and make Grandma feel better. You will want to go to extra efforts today, just to remind yourself not to allow any negative displays. Remind them often, just how special they are in your life. Overcompensating for how badly you feel is perfectly fine if it keeps you on the right track. An ice cream cone shared on the porch couldn't hurt either.

Believe me when I tell you they must think "Grandma is all better" before they leave. They need to know they are not leaving you with the headache you had when they arrived. Communicate how proud you are of how much better they made you feel, so they are satisfied.

Listening intently throughout their childhood will lead to trust as they become young adults. Open communication from the very beginning is critical to building that special bond you desire. Always be there, always listen, and never criticize or judge. If correction needs to be made, initiate it without putting their ideas aside, or reacting in a negative tone. Be a coaching partner; be a perfect Grandma.

7

CONCENTRATING ON EDUCATION

You will educate your grandchild every time you are together, whether you intend to or not. From a very early age, children mimic what they see and absorb everything they hear, good or bad. It will absolutely shock you when something comes up that you thought had long been forgotten.

I recall one day when Emma called her Daddy "stupid", and although it was not done in an angry or ugly manner, she required a "time-out". Her parents are excellent about ending a "time-out" by asking her if she understood what she had done wrong. She replied by saying "stupid" is a mean word, and we shouldn't say it. Okay, success was achieved. She was with me about 6 months later, and we were watching a children's movie when someone used the big bad "stupid" word. She had been relaxing in my lap until then; but promptly sat up, turned to me and said that they needed to go to "time-out". She wanted to know why his Mommy and Daddy had not told him about that ugly word. I agreed with her and we returned to the movie.

My reaction had to continue in the same line with her parents. At that moment I was reinforcing what they were teaching. My agreement let Emma know what her parents taught was correct, validated by Grandma.

Offer to be involved in the future plans for your grandchild's formal education. When Emma was born, her parents planned on home schooling her, and wanted me to be part of that plan. I was excited, with retirement only three years away. My daughter, at the time, had a successful career in an Engineering firm and had not yet entertained the idea of leaving, to become a stay-at-home Mommy.

As the next year passed, they agreed it would be best for Emma if Mommy retired and became available to concentrate on all aspects of her development. So, now the plan had been altered, and I would fall into a lesser role, working as a support to my daughter, who would be her primary educator.

It was a sound plan, and we were all excited as we looked toward her future.

Well, as with all well laid plans, these again changed. Emma's social skills developed rapidly. She was displaying real leadership tendencies. She obviously desired the competition of her peers throughout her day, rather than learning one-on-one. Her parents realized that even the idea of a Co-op was not going to be enough to satisfy Emma. You could see her excitement as she took charge around other children; and her parents wanted to provide her with every opportunity for growth, fearing she would eventually regress if not properly challenged.

Plans A & B had now bitten the dust, and we moved on to plan C. Her parents are the type who will willingly put aside their original ideas if they are presented with something better for Emma. Let me say, right out loud, how lucky Emma is for that. Plan C is a Christian Academy, offering the education we all wish for her. There will be no limits to her development; and she will, no doubt, excel as a leader, with the drive we have witnessed.

Here is the part I need to do. I will want to stay up on what she will be learning for each session, so I can be of assistance where needed. There is nothing more frustrating to a child when they ask for help, then if they are lead in a different direction from what their teacher is presenting. It is easy enough to keep up on their curriculum as you refresh your own mind.

Review where you fit in your grandchild's plans; perhaps you will be needed after school each day, if their Mommy works. What a great opportunity for you. Snack time first, naturally, and then, depending on the age, you will want to review what they were taught that day, and marvel in their success, as you monitor and encourage the preparation of their homework for the next day. This is your opportunity to stay connected, and show them you are interested. Grab every chance you can to share quality time and build a solid bond that will become stronger every day.

What about the rest of their education? Things not addressed in the classroom, can be every bit as important. The social graces will carry them through every possible situation they encounter throughout their lives. Learning proper etiquette will make it a routine style of behavior as they get older. You can routinely incorporate every aspect of the social graces, and they will simply start using them.

Emma is learning how to properly set the table for a meal and she lets me know how wonderful it looks when she is done. Okay, so the napkins are not really straight, but the fork manages to find its way to the napkin every time. I make sure I provide the praise without making corrections. She will become more coordinated as time goes on and the structure of the placements will automatically fall into place, due to practice, and age.

Something as simple as the volume of their voice is an important lesson needed if they are to interact properly. Emma always tells me when she is using her "indoor" voice, since we are not in the yard. That is something I have heard her Mommy express to her as her volume increases at home; and the practice carried over nicely at Grandma's. We have agreed, however, tickles & giggles, and all other uncontrollable laughter does not count.

Practice introductions, with her dolls and animals, so it is not uncomfortable when they are introduced to others. Be certain to coordinate this practice with the way their parents prefer the practice to flow. Continuity is critical in order to eliminate any confusion. I always begin with "Hello, it's very nice to meet you". That way it is simple and easy, and you can add what the parents want.

Always make sure that you remember the age of the child you are working with, and act accordingly. You may even wish to add skills specific to the interests of your granddaughter or grandson. Granddaughters are usually happy to learn simple sewing skills which can develop into highly useful skills later in life, if the desire is there. You may want to let Grandpa handle the car repair training unless you were lucky enough to gain that training on your own. And yes, auto repairs are good for granddaughters as well as grandsons. This Grandma simply has no knowledge to offer in that area. I will rely on Emma's Daddy for that part.

But let's not leave out Mother Nature. You will want to invest in some books that provide information, and pictures, of trees, plants, birds, and even bugs in your local area. Exploration is exciting, and finding a match to something in the yard, in Grandma's books, is a bigger thrill than you could imagine. Take one day specifically for leaves, go to a wooded area such as a park, and find as many different types as you can. When you get home try and match what they found with pictures in the book. Make a display on construction paper, put it into a shadow box and hang it on the wall. A child's pride in accomplishing something they did, just because they wanted to, is quite grand. Another day you could use bark from different trees, or even bugs. These displays work wonderfully for "show-and-tell" at school. Your grandchild will also feel that same pride each time they look at the display on Grandma's wall.

Do you have a pet Grandma? Some of you do, and we have already discussed the best ways to introduce them to your toddler. But, if you are like me, you did not find a need for a pet, until now. A pet is a wonderful reason for your grandchild to come visit. I'm not talking about a yappy little spoiled lap dog who wants nothing to do with your little one. If that's what you already have then you will probably want to put your pet in its kennel or in another room when your, ever so curious, grandchild comes over. Well that's no fun. You will need to begin the doggy training we previously discussed in Chapter 3, so they can learn to be playmates in the near future.

If you are currently without a pet, and are willing to entertain the idea of adding one to your home, you will want to carefully think about your selection. Study the breeds that are known to be gentle with children. Decide whether you prefer an indoor pet, outdoor pet, or one that can handle both. Think about the pet, not just your grandchild, and consider what you will be satisfied with as well. A husky in the southern states is simply cruel; and your pet needs to fit the size of its surroundings. A retriever, for example, has no business in an apartment. Take the time to think through your choices so that you, your grandchild, and your new pet, can be a good, healthy fit.

You will want to make sure your little one understands the importance of respect and love toward their new pet. Remind them this is Grandma's pet, selected specifically with them in mind. As they learn how to interact with each other, you will discover you have found another way to relax and observe while your grandchild visits. Grandma's have physical limits; and playtime in the yard between your pet and grandchild can allow time for you to sit and enjoy that large glass of tea, on the porch, as you watch the delight of their laughter.

I had discussed my plans for a pet with Emma. She understood that Grandma was going to get a puppy in the near future. She asked if it would be a girl, and I told her it would. She then told me she wanted to name her, if that was okay. OMG, what was I to do then? I did not want to refuse such a sweet request. But what did she have in mind? Could I really live with the name she came up with? Come on Grandma, how bad could it be? This is precious Emma, and there is no way I would deny her request. So, being a brave Grandma, I decided I would learn to live with whatever name she provided, and said "I think that would be a wonderful idea. What is her name going to be"? —"Rosie", (and I took a deep sigh of relief).

On the other hand, you may be more inclined to select a kitten, or two. It really doesn't matter as long as you provide a loving pet, and the opportunity to teach your grandchild the joy of loving and caring for an animal. It is something special, to be cherished, forever.

Earlier we discussed the Grandma rules, some of which were related to safety. But, although

rules are rules, and your grandchild is cooperative in following them, do they understand? Do
they realize the rules are based on love? They
need to be what I refer to as "Grandma's Love
Rules". Emma knows that until she is school age,
she is required to sit in the shopping cart, or hold
Grandma's hand at all times, when we are away
from home. When we take a walk, we swing hand-
in-hand, and she is next to the curb, so Grandma
can be next to the street. If we are shopping
where there are no baskets provided, we move
from display to display as she stays by my side.
There is no wondering off allowed, since I am the
only one there watching her. It is not a choice;
it is not up for discussion; it is a "Grandma Love
Rule". Privileges in my home are expanded as she
proves to me she can adhere to the rules I have
established. She announced one day that she did
not need to hold my hand while we were on my
driveway, but she would take my hand again when
we got to the curb. She explained that I could
trust her to stay on the front yard, or the driveway, because she knew how to follow the rules. I
allowed her to prove herself since she had actually made the announcement, as I acknowledged
she was doing what she knew Grandma expected,
and I released her hand (carefully watching her
every move). She needed me to know she could
be trusted.

Emma is quite a social butterfly, as they say, and when we go to the park she immediately finds other children to play with. She knows Grandma is watching and she comes to me periodically to let me know how much fun she is having, and to tell me she loves me. She has been instructed to come only to me, no other adult. She is not allowed to go with a playmate to where that child's parents are, since we do not know them. Please make that one of your rules. You and I both know there are people out there who will lure children to them, by the use of other children. It would be a Grandma's worse nightmare, to have something happen to your grandchild. You are the adult in charge of their safety. Take the responsibility seriously.

Most of what we have covered in this chapter would not fall under, what we normally term as education, but it obviously was. Every moment you spend with your precious grandchild is part of their complete education. They are listening, watching, and learning. Beware Grandma, you are on display.

8

INDEPENDENCE

Oh my goodness, where to begin—the levels of independence are vast. They actually begin at infancy. You remember your own children's fits at that age, yes, in the crib, kicking and crying at something as simple as a diaper change. Your baby didn't mind a wet diaper nearly as much as they minded you changing it. But a dirty diaper, well that was another matter altogether. You would get a wailing demand for your attention, and a clean-up. That, my friend, is independence, or demand for you to pay attention to their needs. They want-ed to clearly display who was going to run this show. Don't let it come to you as a surprise when your ever-so-precious grandbaby gives you the same treatment. Why not, you are obviously someone who loves and cuddles them; you are a sure thing Grandma, just like Mommy and Daddy, to be used for their comfort and desires. They are in the driver's seat, they are in charge, and you know it.

It's understandable because they are incapable of speaking a language we can comprehend at this stage, so demands, in a loud tone, are all they have. Then it is up to you to figure out what is needed, or simply desired. Good luck with that. It should be easy enough; after all, you've been there and done that, all before. You can master this, and be great at it. You are going to be perfect.

Time passes and we enter the crawling stage. Oh my, what a great time to display independence. Your little angel can get from one spot, where you put them, to one that you did not intend them to be. Picking them up and putting them back is extremely unpopular; but you have no choice because you have not had time to properly childproof your home. You are unsure how detailed this process needs to be. Should you latch every single drawer and cabinet? That feels like overkill, but who knows. So you plan on securing only the ones that pose a threat to their safety. Forget the drawer of plastics, or linens, or even placemats and napkins. Believe me, they will quickly discover which ones they can open, and crawl in, or at least empty. Enjoy, this is the simple part of their independence; and besides, it is a development tool. Exploring in a safe environment is something you want to encourage.

Remember that special drawer in my kitchen, the large one near the bottom, full of plastics, just meant to be found by Emma? When she discovered it, and realized she was at liberty to empty everything out, she was thrilled, and entertained for an extended period of time. She never had to be shown where her special drawer was when she came for a visit. She always remembered, and went straight to it. She did not request, or require permission. She took the initiative on her own, learning her independence.

With crawling behind them, they start walking, and a new world of opportunities become available. Getting from place to place is really easy, except for the gates you have strategically placed in office and bedroom doorways. The intent, on your part, was not to keep them from exploration, or from furthering their education, no sir, it was for safety, and your general sanity. Gates, although a great idea, are rarely popular with your budding toddler. Rest assured Grandma, you can avoid being blamed. When Emma would become frustrated with the gates, I would simply agree with her and walk away; and she would follow me, satisfied I suppose. As she became a little older she would say "lift me over Grandma". She had discovered the solution to the irritating gates; and I was her tool to new territories. Unfortunately, I responded with "Grandma can't do that, Sweetie". She never questioned me beyond that; I'm not sure why. I suppose Grandma knows best in these matters.

More time passed and it became obvious the gates were no longer of value. She took me by the hand one day, right over to one of the gates, and said, "Grandma, watch what I can do". She proceeded to give the gate a hearty shove, and down it went. She looked up at me, with all of her pride in tow, and said, "I'm a big girl now Grandma, aren't you surprised?" Naturally, being the perfect Grandma, I hugged and kissed and agreed we no longer needed gates for such a big girl.

I then took her in to the room and explained why there had been a gate, when she was still little. I made sure she knew that since she was now a big girl, I could trust her not to open dresser drawers, etc; and she promised. I showed her each picture on the night stands as well, explaining who each person was, and reminding her to kiss her fingers and place the kiss on each one, in lieu of picking up the picture. The entire process probably took the better part of a half hour and Emma listened intently. I told her if she wanted to see something in that room that I would take her. It has never been a problem. You must take the time with your grandchild to go through the steps and reasons for handling a new adventure, your way. Now, if I am in that room, and she follows me, she tells me all about everything there, and I listen.

But a small child's independence, or attempt at it, can delve into other areas. For example, I had fixed dinner for the two of us, and I made what I knew she would enjoy. She very sweetly thanked me for cooking the dinner and stated each item that she liked; and then announced that she didn't like carrots. I smiled at her and said, "Oh Emma, you are being silly with Grandma, I already knew you liked them, that's why I cooked them", and then I tickled her chin. She smiled back and said, "I was just playing, Grandma", as she proceeded to eat her carrots. This was nothing but a test of her independence. So I asked her if there was something she really did not like very much, so I would know. She didn't have an answer. It was at her bedtime when she said, "Grandma, I don't think I like ants very well, but I still like carrots". Although the two were unrelated, I knew she had been thinking about our conversation, and she was still letting me know she was capable of making a decision on her own, regarding her likes and dislikes. I told her I would never cook ants for dinner, she giggled, and agreed. You will want to encourage them as they become little thinkers, but guide them.

Wardrobes can be a topic all their own. This can be tricky. Their sense of fashion can be questionable, and yet they will try to dictate their choices. I don't believe they always choose what they want to wear as much as they want to be heard, and taken seriously. My daughter had learned to provide options to Emma. She would lay out three options, appropriate for the day, and allow a choice to be made from there. It provided Emma with a certain level of importance and independence, and maintained my daughter's good taste, all at the same time.

I normally purchased 2-3 new outfits in preparation for Emma's visits, and would allow her to select one of them to wear on the trip home. She was only three when we were ending a sleepover and she was ready to pick the outfit to wear. I showed her the outfits and she pointed to the first and announced that it wasn't very cute. Once the shock wore off, I suggested she try it on and look in her mirror. Being the sweetheart that she is, she agreed. All decked out, looking cuter than a button, she told me it still wasn't very cute. So I asked her to try the second outfit. But, before we went any further, she told me she didn't think that one was cute either. I guess the look on my face made her realize I was not prepared for such news, and she said, "But I will wear it if you want me to Grandma". That did it; she was going to give up on her own opinion, just to please me. I hugged her and said that it was not necessary. I told her I would take the two outfits back to the store. Number three was a skirt, instead of shorts, one that would spin, with a top that had sparkles. Her eyes lit up and she declared it a "princess out-fit". We put it on and I told her I thought we had a matching headband, with a bow, in the drawer. We did, it was pink, and she was thrilled. We decided that the next time I shopped for her we would go together. She was beginning to develop a genuine choice in appearance. She was tiring of shorts and wanted to wear skirts. Her sweet attitude proved to me it was not a matter of getting her way; she was genuinely developing an opinion of her own.

In the evening, as we wind down, and are ready for a movie, I allow Emma to make the selection from her shelf of movies. Once she has made a decision, I ask her why she selected that particular movie, and insist on a real answer. She always tells me what it is that made her want to watch it. I get a variety of responses, such as:

- Pooh is silly when he is out of honey
- Tiana is a funny frog, and I like it when she has to eat a bug
- Boo is just like me, she has piggy tails
- Dori speaks whale, and I want to speak whale too
- This movie just makes me feel happy inside

She provides valid reasons for her selection, driven by her age. It made me realize she was not blindly picking a movie; she was making a decision. That's what we want to encourage; and we are given the opportunity every time we are with them.

Have you ever noticed when you take them to the park, or even their church classroom, that they automatically migrate to a particular type of child? They seem to recognize compatibility. Normally it works very well, but on occasion they will not be accepted by someone they have chosen to play with. I have watched Emma try to make a friend, and even heard her ask a child to be her friend, just to see her rejected. She struggles with the rejection, not understanding the reason. That's when guiding them to another child can be helpful. Sometimes the hurt from being pushed away can be painful. That's when you need to assure your grandchild that some children have not been taught to be kind, or to make friends. It never hurts if the parents overhear your conversation. Hugs help too. I like to then do something special for Emma to help put the disappointment behind her. Grandma's love and conversation, and perhaps a dish of frozen yogurt with sprinkles, usually makes life a little better.

Explain to your little one that even parents, and Grandma's, are rejected sometimes. We cannot make another person be nice, but, we can still be nice in return. When all else fails there is Grandma, "who loves you bunches and bunches".

With each month that passes you will hear more "I can do it myself". Although it is not necessarily true, they want it to be. Frustration will be witnessed as they try to do the things they have not yet mastered, but you can assist, at least as much as they will allow. When Emma was learning to put her night gowns on, she only needed help getting started. I would put it over her head and she would take it from there. On occasion she would find it difficult to get her hand lined up with the opening to the sleeve, and become upset. I didn't take over, saying "I can help you" or "I can do that for you"; because she believed she was capable of doing it herself. The first time she had grave difficulty with the sleeve, I told her it was okay because I thought her hand just got the "silly hiccups" and forgot how to jump into the sleeve. "I will speak with that hand and tell it to behave and to do what it is supposed to do". With that said, I spoke to the hand, and, ever so slightly slid the sleeve closer so it was lined up, and ready. Then I assured Emma that her hand would be nice now. She proceeded and accomplished her goal. She was thrilled with herself as a result, and I provided the praise for a job well done.

The idea is to allow them to learn new things, feel as if they are doing most of it all on their own, while guiding the learning process. Learning something new is an adventure and allows a sense of pride in their independence.

But caution is called for, as your sweet grand-child takes on the world, unafraid. Gently holding their hand as you cross the street has never been an issue before; but now, quicker than you could imagine, they may break free and dart off without you. It isn't a matter of not behaving; it is a matter of letting you know they are now big enough to go to the neighbor's without help. Be prepared in advance, because this is surely coming. Be telling your little one that although you realize they are getting big, you still need them to do some things with Grandma, so you are both safe. Cars do not always stop, just because they are supposed to. Tell them that as soon as you have both watched for traffic and crossed the street together; you will trust them to go from the bottom of the driveway, all the way to the front door, without holding hands. Once they arrive, provide praise for them, since they can be trusted to do exactly as Grandma said.

If you suddenly find defiance showing up, remember it is also part of the package. Work with it. The only way your grandchild will learn is by exploration, and using their emotions is part of the process. They learned to use tears, early on, for sympathy. Oh, come on now—you don't really believe that all of those sweet tears were due to sadness or pain, do you? Some were only because you would give in, and perhaps, just perhaps, let a second cookie make its way to their little hand, sweetly waiting. Watch for the defiance and make sure you remain in control. I have been known to simply sit on the floor and ask if Emma was okay, or explain that Grandma didn't understand what was wrong. Sometimes just saying, "Can you tell Grandma what you are trying to do" will give them a chance to talk to you, and let you know what is really going on. Scolding them is absolutely the worst thing you could do at a time like this. You will have ignored what they need. They are obviously upset and these emotions are confusing them. If they feel ignored they will become angry or withdraw. Everyone will lose, and you will never know what your grandchild was trying to accomplish. Perhaps you could have been helpful.

At one point Emma let me know she wanted privacy in the bathroom, if she had extra business to be handled—you know, she needed to do "#2". I wasn't sure I could trust her not to lock the door, and I didn't have a key. I readily agreed to her request, and as I shut the door I instructed her to call out to me when she needed me to come back. She agreed, I shut the door, and held the knob so it couldn't be locked. She never caught on. When she called for me I simply waited a few seconds before responding, so she would think I was down the hall. It worked beautifully.

Then there is the true test of a Grandma's love and patience. Imagine yourself in the kitchen, allowing your precious little cook to mix the pancake batter. The egg breaks a bit prematurely, slides right through those sweet little fingers, across the chair, and down on the floor. Realizing there is a mess to clean up; she gets down, tipping the bowl of pancake mix on to the table, which she promptly brushed to the floor. You assure her you will clean it up, but— Oh no, this darling, budding chef is developing her own independence, remember? She will do it for you. Off she goes to the counter to get the dishtowel, which she uses to spread the mixture into a sticky compound, while stepping in it as she works. It is then carried into the carpeted area, so she can check on the cartoon she is missing. Where do you step in, when do you take over? How much more can possibly go wrong? Oh, quit panicking; I was only making it up to scare you.

The point of the story is to remind you that although you want to encourage your grandchild to develop their independence, you will need to retain control. They are small, unskilled, and require your protection and guidance. Be attentive, loving, and allow them to believe that they are fully in charge, as they go about the learning process. But Grandma, watch them closely.

9

DO AS I SAY, NOT AS I DO

We make a great many rules, for a great many reasons, as we care for our grandchild. We try to do as their parents instruct in order to provide harmony in their training; and adhere to the schedules they are accustomed to at home. We provide instructions for their safety, and carefully watch over them. So far it doesn't seem all that difficult. We have learned what to tell them, so they can develop their play habits and general good manners. At this point you probably believe you are right on track, and actually doing a pretty good job. Go ahead, pat yourself on the back, and give yourself an "atta-boy" for your success. Be aware, you are doing so well that you may not see what they see. That's right; they see what you do all the time.

When you tell your grandchild it is bath time, they trot off to the tub where their toys await them. If you suggest a game, they know to pick up the stuffed animals and go select the game of their choice. You have accomplished a great deal so far. Your grandchild loves coming over, and the two of you have found a real continuity, with the flow of activities in your home working like a well oiled machine, with only an occasional snag. When something new arises you manage it well and make it work in your favor.

Visits are so comfortable that you are now at risk of letting your guard down. Children watch what we do routinely, all of the time. And since they love us, they will emulate what we do, so they can be more like us. Did it ever occur to you that although we tell them not to do something, we follow by breaking our own rule? Let me provide you with an example someone gave me years ago. I wish I could remember who it was, because I would give them a prize.

- You tell a child that it is dangerous to pull a cord out of an electrical socket, or to plug anything into that socket.
- You then go to the kitchen, unplug the toaster, and plug in the blender.

What have you just done? You told your sweet little one never to do such a thing, because it is dangerous, then you do it yourself. What do they think now? Was Grandma wrong? Is it really okay since she does it? Is Grandma going to get hurt since it is dangerous? Why did Grandma tell me not to do it? I'm big now, and Grandma can trust me to do the things she does. You have told them to do "as you say" but not "as you do". You have now managed to confuse your grandchild, completely. Unfortunately, they may just make their own decision going forward, since your message makes no sense at all——Oops!

Telling a child that something is dangerous is not a good enough reason for not doing it. There are times when additional information is needed. There are some things that must only be done by "very careful" grown-ups. You cook on back burners in order to prevent little hands from being burned, but you can take the opportunity to explain your intent. You can simply add that hot objects need to stay in the back because a burn would hurt, and Grandma is here to make sure her sweetheart in not hurt; and accidents can happen if we are not careful. Explain that there are some things that need to be done only by Mommy, Daddy, or Grandma. Then go into all the new things they have recently accomplished, that all of the grown-ups agree are safe and okay to do. Emphasize how proud you are that you can trust them to remember the "safety rules".

Table manners should not be a problem for you; after all, most of us are well versed on proper etiquette and have no issue with our grandchild copying our talents. And rarely would we display any negative remarks or actions, while out shopping. Uh oh, "rarely" is not good. No doubt, it will be when you have your sweet one with you that someone will cut in line, in front of you, at the mall. You have been waiting a very long time, your grandchild is tired and hungry, the woman who cut in line is arguing about the sale item which is no longer on sale, and she insists on seeing the Manager. You can't move to another line because that clerk is out helping someone, on the floor, instead of behind the check-out counter where she belongs. The Manager arrives and can't seem to satisfy the woman. Your patience has ended, and you say something "slightly" ugly, to make a point, as you dump your items on the counter, and promptly leave. Unfortunately, the items you have just left behind were for your grandchild.

Now what? If you are still carrying an attitude, your little one can certainly feel it. This is something they are unaccustomed to, from Grandma. They may become completely silent at this point, being a bit frightened. On the other hand, they may wonder why they are being punished. Remember, you just left their purchase behind. What do you imagine was going through their mind as they witnessed rude words, especially in a harsh or loud tone? And will your frustration control your actions after you leave the store? Will you still go to lunch as you previously promised, or go home to pout? What a mess you've just made.

We emphasize how to treat playmates, how to speak with people we encounter, how to be polite at all times; and then, in a matter of a few minutes, we erase it all. The old adage that "actions speak louder than words" is true. Depending on the depth of your anger with the situation, the result could be tears, and a ruined day. A grandchild is sensitive to your words and actions. And although nothing in the last scenario was directed at anyone other than the clerk, or the situation, it had the greatest effect on the one person you did not intend to hurt. With the damage done, you certainly don't want your frustration to continue to control you. This needs an immediate band-aid. Stop outside the store, cover your mouth, put a twinkle in your eye, and say, "Oh my goodness, Grandma should not have done that". Laugh a little, to help break the ice, and follow with, "That was a no-no". Assure them that Grandma will not do that again, and let them know grown-ups make mistakes sometimes, and that you are sorry. You will want to make the remainder of the day all positive. Now, if the purchases left behind were promised items for them, you will still need to rectify that issue right away. The down side to all of this, although repaired to some degree, is that they will still remember it. It is a side of Grandma they had not experienced before, and they will watch for it in the future.

Another area to watch carefully is your attitude in the car. Small children love to sing and be silly in their car seats. It does no harm, and they are simply being children. Don't become "short" with them, or allow their entertainment to frustrate you. You are then at risk of reactions toward other drivers. They are all ears and will gladly repeat the words you direct to others. Just be aware that your words will be carried home, and you will have failed "Test # whatever". You forgot about the tests didn't you? They never end, and you could blow this deal at any time. You will be watched until your little darling is fully grown.

Emma and I had been shopping and witnessed a Grandma, who was harsh with her small grandchild, even going so far as to tell him to "shut up". Emma watched without a word, and I guided our cart elsewhere, to get away from the situation. I addressed the issue immediately so she knew I was aware of what happened. I told Emma that Grandma was unhappy for the child. Emma stated that the little boy's Grandma just didn't love him; and then she hugged me and said. "But my Grandma sure loves me". Naturally, with my heard swelling, I responded in kind. She had seen, and heard, what lessons could not have taught. It was the reality of what she believed to be a lack of love, not just a bad mood. I wondered if the little boy felt the same message that Emma did.

I have seen adults, in charge of a small child, walking through a parking lot, with the child following behind. They have probably taught the child to watch both ways before crossing the street, but left them to their own defenses in a parking lot full of cars. Those children are certainly receiving mixed messages. The actions of their parents have erased the safety warnings they tried to teach. Mommy did not check for cars as she strolled toward an opening trunk, so why would their child? If we tell them to watch for cars, let's take their hand, or have them hold on to the shopping cart, and actually watch for cars. Let them see that your actions match what you have told them to do. Then remind them, each time, why it is done, to set the pattern.

Now, here is one that will make you think. How often do we tell them to put their toys away after they are through playing with them; pretty much all of the time, right? What about the example we provide in return? Your grandchild has been good about following your rules; but what about Grandma? When you are through reading that book you are so interested in, do you put it away? No, you tell them you aren't finished yet; but it appears to them that you are, because you have left it by the chair and gone on to something else. They may remind you of that fact the next time you want them to put something away. They may announce that they aren't finished playing with it yet. The same may happen when you leave your shoes beside the recliner or a coffee cup on the counter. They are observing your actions all the time. Sure, they heard your rules, and for the most part they understood the lessons, but remember, actions are reality to them.

When you ask a child to finish what is on their plate, be sure yours is clean as well. If they cannot have a cookie until they finish their dinner, follow the same rule for everyone else at the table.

Little eyes see all, and little minds are absorbing what they see. They love you Grandma, and look up to you for guidance, and example of what to do. Don't allow your actions to work against your carefully designed lessons. Be consistent with what you teach so they do not receive mixed messages. Believe me when I tell you that the message which will remain solidly in their precious memory will be the one attached to an action.

10

FAMILY PHOTOS AND
MEMORIES

As parents, with our first child, we took more photos than anyone could believe. Our infant could not make a move without the snap of the camera. We were diligent about printing multiple copies of each picture and placing them in several types of albums. That's what good parents did, right? That nonsense went on for months, and then, due to a lack of available time to work on the albums, we spread the pictures out a bit. Over the next year or so the photos were only once or twice a day, and then they were spaced to perhaps one a week. We soon became so involved in the actual raising of our child that we were too tired to work on the albums, and they made their way to a drawer. Shortly they were mislabeled for age, as we tried to recall what month they would have been taken, based on the outfit they wore. Then if we sort of managed to get through the first year of pictures, we were certainly lost with the next year. Life was far too busy to stop and work on photo albums. Reality set in and we took fewer pictures, learned to date them, and put them in "the drawer" for someday, when life would be a little slower, and we could actually work on our albums.

This is where you have the advantage. You are fully aware that an infant is not going to change dramatically between photos taken twice a week. And, as the months go on, you can select pictures by actual things they do, so there is a memory attached to each one. I began by making the first album encompass only the first year. It was a scrapbook which allowed me to add stickers and cute labels to each page. That album was intended for momentous occasions such as holidays, special outings, first bath, etc. It began with her birth and ended at her first birthday party. The next scrapbook was also for a one year period, ending with her second birthday. After that, each one was for a two year period and was only for holiday photos.

Don't get me wrong, I took more photos than that, and Emma's parents supplied me with plenty of pictures that were taken of cute moments at home. Those were placed in my "daily" albums. You know, those generic albums that hold bunches of pictures and have space to add a little note beside each one. You never get behind on those, because as soon as you print a set of photos, you date them and load them into the album. No need for remembering when they were taken because it was within the past month and each picture tells its own story. One could be "a day at the zoo" or "helping Daddy wash the car". No guess work and you are finished with the newest group of pictures, ready for another batch.

When it is a couple of weeks between visits, as it can be, or I know Emma has been under the weather, and I miss her more than usual, I pour a cup of coffee, pick up an album, and just go through it. You can't really do that with a drawer full of loose pictures. It brings me close to her again, and helps me wait for our next time together.

Scrapbooks on the other hand, are more of a display. Your local hobby store has everything you need to decorate each page, and tell a story behind a single picture. This is more of a cold weather project for me. I plan for a day alone, perhaps a couple of cups of hot apple cider, and my scrapbook. Because the number of pictures is limited, you can easily have them dated on the back, and put in a plastic bin along with your decorations, to make it perfect. I intend to continue these until Emma is grown, and give them to her as a wedding gift, or perhaps as she gets her first home.

Something else I do, probably more enriching than the albums, is my diary. I purchased a group of small, lined books, for notes; with a delicate design on the outside. Each book is hard covered, and the same size. I began the first diary with the excitement of learning I was going to be a Grandma. I dated each page as something significant happened, such as when the nursery was painted in anticipation of Emma's arrival. Each page was labeled by the day of the week, and actual date. Once Emma was born, entries were only when we were together. I would write about what we did, where we were, and anything cute I wanted to associate with that day.

Once I had filled the first diary; I dated it and began the second. I get great satisfaction knowing I record every time we are together. Some entries were surprise visits to my office to take me to lunch; and some covered several pages, if it was due to a sleep-over. Sometimes I pick up a diary and just flip to a page to see what happened that day. It brings the day back to life and floods my mind with the entire experience. And you, Grandma, can tell your grandchild the first time they read you a story or spoke whale with you while watching a favorite movie, or called you Grandma and brought tears of joy to your eyes.

Parents don't have the luxury of maintaining albums or diaries like we do. After all, they are living all of it 24-7, and resting when they get a free minute, or trying to quickly catch up on everything they had to put aside when their child was requiring their undivided attention. Our catch-up time is immediate, as soon as our sweet, loving grandchild goes home. We have plenty of time to re-group for the next visit, but Mommy, well she has only brief moments.

Your home should always reflect the importance of family in your life. Grandchildren love to go from picture to picture and tell you who each person is. I remember when I was given a picture of her family, large enough to frame and display. The picture was of Emma and her parents during the holidays, not just a snapshot, but a portrait. When she discovered it in the bookcase, where her other pictures are displayed, she proudly stated "Grandma, this is my family". She was thrilled with the picture and asked if she could please hug it, if she was really careful. Naturally I said yes. Some of her favorite pictures are from when she was very small; but because they are framed and out, she explains each one to me, nearly every time she comes. We move from room to room and she tells me who each person is, even if she has never met them. She is remembering what I have told her. "This is my Uncle Dickie who is married to Aunt Gloria, and they are really nice". She actually has no idea how they are related to her, but she wants me to believe she does; and besides, Grandma told her once, or twice. There is special warmth to a home with pictures, and it can be felt by the reactions of a child. So if you have not framed and displayed your grandchild's pictures, you need to get busy. Make sure they know how important they are to you, and that you want everyone who comes to visit, to see them also.

On one of our recent sleep-over's it was raining and our outside plans were spoiled. So I pulled out photo albums of my life as a child, which she could hardly believe. Then we moved on to see Mommy as a baby, and later as a child. Although it was obviously difficult for her to imagine, there we were in pictures, making it true. I even told her stories to go along with the pictures, which delighted her even more.

As time passes you will want to let your grandchild begin an album of their own, for photos of their good times at Grandma's house. Let them take some pictures of you, and you take some of them. Work together with sticker labels and artwork that can easily be attached. It will end up nice enough, and they will have done most of the work themselves. Add to it every few times they come over so you maintain the interest; but stop as soon as they tire of the project. It is meant to be fun, not a chore. Do not address it as "working on our scrapbook" but as "building our memory book", and, by all means, have a snack at the same time. It will be something that reminds them of Grandma's, since it was your special project together.

We all know how much a child enjoys having a story read to them; but they also love telling stories. During their early years it is even more fun if they tell you a story about something they have done, rather than you reading or telling one. Take out one of the albums and find a snapshot of them during an activity; and ask them to tell you all about that day. I showed Emma a picture of her with her Daddy, standing beside his riding mower. When I asked what they had been doing, she proceeded to go into a lengthy story about helping her Daddy clean the yard. They were raking sticks to be piled up for burning, as they planned to roast marshmallows. She provided every tiny detail about how big the sticks were, and how some were crooked. She even explained how careful a little girl has to be when cooking something over a fire. From there she fully educated me on fire safety. We even discussed what to do, and not to do, around the "big tractor" if the engine is turned on. I don't believe anything was forgotten in the story; and she was delighted when she would remember an additional topic to add, related to that day. The more she told, the more exciting the story became for her. She was "in her element" as they say, and it was all because of a single snapshot. Imagine the hours of entertainment you could enjoy if you took turns telling stories, based on photos from a family album.

You can always incorporate an activity with a story being told. Thinking back, I could have offered Emma a plastic rake and suggested we rake the sticks and leaves in Grandma's yard. Next time we share a "photo story", as we call them, I will add a game or activity, just to see how well it works. We could have just gone through the house and counted all the pictures that had Daddy in them. That too would have been a fun activity for her, to share with Grandma.

While they are learning to take their own set of photos, most will not be good enough to print. Allow them to take plenty since you can always delete the bad ones. Print those that are decent so that the next time they come, you can actually show them how wonderful their pictures turned out, even if you have to add a few of your own. You will need to be ready with scrapbook stickers, album and pages, just in case they want to get started. "We will have to do it another time" just because you were not prepared, won't work. When

they are excited about something that you have
introduced, you need to be ready to move forward.
You will want to make it your priority for the day,
no matter what you had actually planned to do. You
are "the best", remember? And at some point, they
will want to take their completed project home to
show Mommy and Daddy their accomplishment. It
may only be partially done, you may have had additional pages you were going to add, or special ideas
to make it a real work of art, but wait—they think
it's done, so it is! Praise them for how beautifully it
turned out, and allow them to take it home, realizing they may need to be a little older before taking
the scrapbooking project serious. Who cares; you
are always going to be Grandma, and there will
be many opportunities ahead of you. Take a picture of your proud artist, holding the "completed"
album, and save it for your own memory book to
be recalled in the future.

Let's not forget, we will want to encourage them
to collect pictures of their pets, if they have them,
Mommy and Daddy, favorite dolls and stuffed animals, or anything else that is important to them.
Not only will they need the pictures for their next
album; but they will need them for the next "photo
story" time with Grandma. You may want to invest
in a throw-away camera at first and later gradu-
ate to a real one, as they get older. Speak about
it often and ask how much fun they are having.

Inquire who, or what, they took recent pictures of; and explain that when the camera is full, you will have the pictures made for them. It can be fun to go together to drop off the camera and return later in the day to pick up the envelope full of actual pictures. If most are poor, simply explain that it is difficult to take pictures sometimes; but that with practice, and help from Grandma, they will get better ones next time. Then hand them a new replacement camera so they can start over; guide them and witness their improvement.

Photos bring back the yesterdays that fade from our memories. They refresh the stories that were almost forgotten, and make them new again. I believe everyone enjoys remembering the good time they had in the past. I know I do, and so does Emma.

11

BECOME CREATIVE

It should now be obvious to the parents that you can be trusted to follow their guidelines while you are in charge of your grandchild. You have managed to pass the initial "Tests" at this point. You feel like you can relax more, because the rules have been accepted by this time, and everything seems to flow pretty well during the visits.

Enjoy yourself; this isn't going to last. You cannot continue to offer the same activities every time they come to stay. They are developing into creative little people, with ideas of their own. Some of the initial games will no longer be of interest, and will need to be replaced with something new. Being given crayons and a box to color on, worked really well when they were 2 years old, but I'm here to tell you that a 4 year old would prefer color books, or perhaps even water colors as an alternative. So although the basic idea of coloring may still be interesting, the way it's presented will need to progress, just as your grandchild does. And you, Grandma, need to be ready for the challenge.

Too often I have heard Grandma's tell me about week-ends where they surprised their grandchild with a couple of new movies, to keep them entertained. Now don't get me wrong, movies can be fun, and are wonderful as the day comes to an end and it's time to unwind; but don't use movies as a way to "kill time" during the day. The object of having time together is to actually "have time together". You can manage your bed making, meal preparations, kitchen clean-up, etc, while being entertained by your grandchild. The memories related to having a "helper" while doing routine chores can be everlasting. Who cares if the bed pillows are out of order, really? Make stay-over weekends special, for both of you. Plan in advance; and make sure you think of things that are physical, not stagnant, as in front of a TV or computer, during the daylight hours.

I made a list of activities, all I could think of, by age category. Before Emma would come for the week-end, I would refer to the list and select more activities than we could possibly do, in order to have options; and made note of the weather. Some week-ends allowed for outdoor activities the entire time; but if it was going to rain, I would plan more indoor activities. Your list will need to be designed specifically with your little one in mind. You already know their particular likes and dislikes by now, so that will give you a start. Be creative; list things that "could" be of interest. Children love to be introduced to new games and activities.

Think of safety factors as well. If one of the items is going to a theme park you will certainly want the parents' approval. On the other hand, if you are going on a guided tour to an ice cream factory, where free ice cream is the end result, I doubt it would require prior permission. It is still a good idea to let the parents know what your plans are, outside of your home, so they can provide their blessing, and you can climb the ladder of favored relatives.

Too often we ask our little ones if they want to do something, and because they don't realize what it entails, they will simply say "no" and it is eliminated from the list. That would be a mistake on your part. Remember you are the one in charge of the week-end, and need to guide the activities. Instead of saying "do you want to see how ice cream is made?" you can say, "We are going to the great big ice cream factory today to see them make ice cream—and they are going to give us some to eat".

It becomes a simple fact; this is what we are going to do today, followed by a treat you already know they like. Or, you can plan an activity by saying "Oh my goodness, we need to get our boots on, hurry, I have a surprise for you". They will be delighted at the idea of a surprise, and this one includes boots, it must be fun. I thought of that idea one day after a rain, and knew my driveway would be covered with nice puddles, just right for jumping and splashing. You could even create puddles if you need to, with the garden hose. And really, have you ever met a child who didn't like puddles?

Walks, for the purpose of finding things on a list, as you would on a scavenger hunt, can be a wonderful challenge. Make a list, simple enough it can be mastered, and head out. You could have even pre-planned for items to be hidden and located later. If you are in a rural area you will want to remember which tree you put the orange ball under; feeling confident it would still be there to be found the next day. If, on the other hand, you live in a sub-division, it is more likely the orange ball will be found by someone else, and be gone before you get there. Your items to be hidden may need to be in areas you had pre-arranged with willing neighbors, like under a particular shrub. The preparation can actually be as much fun as the walk and hunt. Remember, it is a game to be played together, as a team. That way you can gently guide them toward the goal each time, still allowing them to find the item. If the orange ball is under the shrub in the back corner of the neighbor's yard, you can say, "I will look under these bushes while you look under those". They will be delighted they were able to find what Grandma couldn't.

Sometimes a game you had planned is altered as your grandchild's imagination leads you off in another direction. You could be in the middle of an outdoor activity when your little one lies back on the grass, perhaps after chasing a ball and falling down. Rather than getting up to kick the ball back to you, they realize there are animals in the wonderful puffy white clouds above. Take the opportunity to lie down beside them, to see what they see; pointing out more animals, or a boat perhaps. I hope you are not one of those Grandmas who is more concerned about her perfectly formed hair-do than the bonding moment you are about to share by laying beside your grandchild in order to count fish in the clouds. Get your priorities in order, and enjoy the moment.

Your list can also be geared toward seasonal activities. Most children love to prepare for a holiday. I love to begin decorating my home about a month prior to the actual holiday, and I count on Emma to be a big part of the activity. You will want to make it a time planned event. For example,

I told Emma, when it was time to decorate for Halloween, that right after lunch and a little rest, we would begin. The rest was obviously brief, due to her excitement. We pulled out the bins full of fall decorations, and she checked each one to determine if it was intended specifically for Halloween, or if it was for Thanksgiving, or just a fall seasonal item. Every time she found a pumpkin she knew she could get that one out; and perhaps a funny laughing ghost, or silly scarecrow. She announced, each time she located a pilgrim, or turkey, that it was a Thanksgiving decoration, to be used later. She knew she would be returning for that decorating day as well, after all it was becoming our tradition. Grandma cannot decorate without Emma.

I made suggestions where each item would go, or I would say, "These always go on the coffee table", and she always agreed. She would often ask for permission to carry the item, and I made sure it was okay. If something was delicate I would simply say "I will carry that one so that you can carry the very special one". It would be one that was either not breakable, or not that important, in the event of an accident. It made the item appear to be special and I would ask her if she could carry it very carefully, or let her know I knew she could be trusted to take good care of it for Grandma, which she always did. She was obviously proud that Grandma trusted her.

One item, which was to be placed in that small window beside the front door, broke. You recall that window; it is where I put decorations that Emma is allowed to hold, or carry around when she wants. This time it was a wooden display of pumpkins, with a dangling leaf. The leaf was attached by a small wire, which was old and worn out, and simply broke as it was handled. Emma looked up at me as if she had failed to take care of something I trusted her with. My reaction was critical at this point, and I said, "I'm surprised that silly leaf didn't fall off last year. Do you think we should try to put it back on, or just leave it off? Grandma thinks it looks better without the leaf." She immediately displayed relief and agreed it was better without the leaf, going promptly to the trash to discard it. No more was said about the situation until that evening, during story time. She interrupted our story, turned to me, and said she was sorry she had broken my decoration. I assured her that she didn't break it; it was old and just fell apart. "But you trusted me to take really good care of it"; and I told her she did. I explained that when I need her to take care of something, all she has to do is be careful not to throw it, or pull it apart. If it breaks by accident then that is okay. I told her that Grandma could tell she was being careful. And besides, even if it fell to the floor and broke, Grandma would not be upset, because accidents happen to everyone. She hugged my neck, told me she loved me, and said "that silly leaf was old". I agreed and we returned to our story.

Holidays also offer the opportunities for projects such as pumpkin decorating with markers. I avoid carving while Emma is small, due to safety factors, and besides, you can always take a pumpkin pie later and explain it was made from the inside of her pumpkin. A dab of whipped cream, and you will be quite popular.

Emma's Mommy and Daddy always provide the Thanksgiving celebration in their home, for all of the extended family. They have the skills and talents required to make everything perfect; and it also gives everyone the chance to see Emma for the day. If you will be spending a holiday with the parents of your grandchild, it is a wonderful idea to plan a special project that they can take home for the celebration. It gives them a sense of participation and pride. Last year I got felt turkey cut-outs, and with the assistance of her Grandma, Emma placed fall stickers on each and we added family member's names so they could be used as name tags for the dining table. Everyone made over them, and Emma.

All of the holidays, and birthdays, can be a big part of your list because they normally excite the children. Create your own traditions that you share with your grandchild over the years. You may want to make a Christmas decoration each year, and date it. The hobby stores have a boat-load of ideas along that line. I should buy stock—I'm there all the time.

Your grandchild will learn that there are things they can do with you for each holiday, because it is your special time with them. A sleep-over near July 4 just calls for something to eat that is red, white and blue. Whether it is a carefully decorated cup-cake, jello, or a bowl of blueberries and strawber-ries tossed in vanilla ice cream, it doesn't matter; it is the colors that are important, and the tradition that has been established at Grandma's house. You are the one setting these traditions, while your grandchild is small, and they will be memories to last forever. Make sure they are always happy times, without irritation of things going wrong, or hurt feelings of any kind. These are the times you set aside to make your little one laugh with joy, as they show you how much love they are capable of sharing. Treat yourself to wonderful memories every time you are together.

Movies, as I have stated previously, are not intended to occupy the time of your grandchild so that you can do other things. They are intended for quiet times. I like to offer a movie after lunch when Emma needs to rest, although she would dis-agree. Once her tummy is full, and we have made a trip to the potty, she knows it is movie time. If she realized it was so she could rest she would surely object. She picks the movie she wants and we selects where we are going to sit together. On occasion she will want to lie on the couch with a dolly and a blanket. If that is the case, I sit in a chair nearby so she knows I'm there, although I will not necessarily remain after she falls asleep. If she chooses to be in my lap, in the recliner, I obviously remain as long as she sleeps. We may chat at the beginning of the show, but little by little, I reduce the volume and stop speaking except to respond to her, quietly. Normally the only other time we watch a movie is after her bath, before bed time. It can only be a partial movie due to time restraints, so we skip to the parts we like the best.

As an exception to the rule, there have been rainy days when, during the day, we want an "action" movie, where we can join the activities. "Jungle Book" is a favorite because of the music, dancing, and marching. There would be no resting during that movie. "Snow White", as well, requires me to play the wicked queen, as Emma plays the princess; and there is also a section of enthusiastic dancing we always have to join. Napping would never be considered during the dancing or the "Hi-Ho" marching scene with the seven dwarfs.

You must make the decisions as you go; but never use a movie as a baby sitter. After all, this time that you have requested, is for fun with your little one. You should actually want to be involved with them the entire week-end, savoring every cute activity or conversation.

And don't forget one of the most popular activities, at least for little girls, is playing dress-up. You can do this for hours, being different story book characters, especially if you have a full length mirror. You will need to remember which voice to use for each one because you certainly don't want to mix up the voice of the wicked queen when you are suddenly playing the part of the handsome prince. And heaven forbid the voice of Randall, in "Monsters, Inc", would sound anything like Sully or Boo.

I will admit that I am unfamiliar with play choices for little boys; but would imagine "Toy Story" or "Cars" would be involved as popular movies during the toddler years. Being creative with the characters of those movies would be as easy as with "Snow White". You are the director of fun while they are with you, and the possibilities are unlimited. You have had years to practice being creative, and Grandma's are the best at it.

The one thing I can assure you, as I said earlier, is that as they get older, the initial entertainment ideas will need to upgrade to new ones, more attuned to their new interests. Don't allow Grandma's house to become boring, or simply be an extension of the routine they have at home.

It needs to continue to be special, and fun. They need to look forward to going to Grandma's. Home is for regular living, doing chores, feeling safe and loved as they grow up. Grandma's is for love of a different kind, one that requires only love in return. There is no room for schedules that are unpopular, food that is only nourishing (verses nourishing and fun), expectations that are difficult to meet, or limitations on good times and cookies. The love offered by Grandma is the kind only a Grandma knows how to give. It is fuzzy warm, sweet beyond measure, forgiving every time, unconditional, and theirs alone. That's the love of a "Perfect Grandma".

12

JUGGLING YOUR TIME

My time, because I'm a widow, can be spent, for the most part, with Emma; at least that's my plan. She's my "favorite activity" and I like nothing better than to be with her. Anytime her parents call and ask me to come to the house, or baby sit for the evening, or anything else that involves Emma, I try to say yes; even if I need to cancel previous plans already in place. That's my option; that's my right. I live alone and make all the rules, with no one else to consider.

You, on the other hand, may be part of a grandparent team. You can't always drop everything, pick up your purse, and head out the door. You and Grandpa may have plans, or simply want to be alone for a day of relaxation. And anyway, you would want to consult with him before agreeing to an instant request to take your little one. It is not a matter of less love, obviously, but sometimes arrangements need to be made in advance.

And then there are those of you who are involved in outside activities, scheduled activities, such as church groups or club meetings. After all, you never intended on retiring and sitting at home with nothing on the agenda. If you are involved in a weekly study group you really can't skip several of the sessions and expect to get the desired benefit of the series; you simply lose out on too much. The study groups are something you missed when you were working, and you promised yourself that when you retired you would become serious about attending; and you really want to keep that promise to yourself.

Perhaps you are part of a bridge club that meets on Tuesday mornings; the girls count on you showing up, every time. It's one of your favorite social events and you look forward to it every week. The conversations are fun, the friendships are strong, and the lunch that follows is even better. Besides how are you expected to keep abreast of the latest scandal in the neighborhood if you miss a Tuesday? OMG—you could become the topic of the day. You can't risk that. With all kidding aside, you are simply not available on Tuesdays, and you need the parents to understand.

You will now need to start juggling your time. You can handle this, you are smart and clever. So here we go.

You want to be with your grandchild at every opportunity you are given; but you want your life as well. Your fear is that if you turn their parents down too often, they will stop asking you and automatically turn to someone else, someone more reliable. Your children probably already know what you planned for your retirement. They already understand that you will be involved with friends, clubs and group activities that will require a great deal of your time. It's really no different than when you worked; you were unavailable during certain hours of the day. Well, you still are, except the hours are broken up differently now. Let them know what times you are available; and offer to take your little one on a specific date that works well for you. I guarantee that your grandchild's "structured" parents will be happy to make a plan for you, as they look forward to a grown-up evening, or week-end. Being with your grandchild does not require spontaneity; it can work on a schedule just as well. The idea is to be together when you can enjoy them, and you are free of any other obligations, allowing you to dedicate your full time and attention to their needs.

Perhaps you are lucky enough to travel extensively during your retirement years. You have earned the time, planned and saved, invested wisely, forever it seems, so that you could enjoy all the luxuries of retirement. So here you are retired, and ready to begin traveling. When you started making your plans years ago, you didn't think about anything except the two of you. Your children would be grown and on their own, self reliant, and you would be completely free of all obligations. After all, you raised them well, and felt fully confident they would be successful adults. You were right; they can handle their own lives now, without your assistance, for the most part. But wait, you didn't think about the fact there could be grandchildren. And if you did, you didn't consider they would pull on your heart strings and take over your world with their sweet smiles. But here you are, a Grandma, completely smitten by your little darling. You want to love on your grandchild 24-7, as we all do; but you also want to go and play, just as you dreamed, all those years.

Rest assured, you can still do this. You need to make sure everyone knows your itinerary as you plan a trip, each and every time; then pack and go. Oh yes, by the way, you remember that little thing they call technology? Well, that's going to give you the ability to stay continually connected to your family. You can communicate with your

grandchild, and even see the little darling, anytime you want. Face to face stories, and giggles,
are yours for the asking. You can designate a particular time if that works best for the type of trip
you are on, or just make it happen as you can. I
assure you that your grandchild will be thrilled to
see you as often as you call, especially if you have
something fun to tell them. Always remind them
how much you miss them, send a big hug, and tell
them you love them. It can be especially fun if you
name your hugs, depending on where you are at
the time. Select something local to that area, tell
them about it, and name your hug appropriately.

You could also make them a small photo album
to bring back for them; you know, one of the soft
covered ones that they can carry around. It will
give them a chance to re-live the calls as they look
through their own "memory" album. They will not
mind you taking your next trip because the tradition can easily continue, like a Grandma game.
Remember, children love traditions, and especially games.

Traveling, or outside activities, are not the only
reasons we need to be experts in juggling our time.
It would stand to reason that you are probably
not the only Grandma in the picture. In my case,
there is also a Nana and a Gramm; and included
with Nana, there is Pawpaw. So, all toll, there are
four of us. Fortunately we all get along well, and

actually enjoy each other's company. When we gather for occasions where Emma's parents have a celebration or dinner for the extended family, we all allow Emma to make her rounds between us. We each know how much she loves us, and she is in her glory to have access to everyone at the same time, not to mention her Aunts and Uncles.

We also understand that Emma will be with another Grandma at different times. I believe the others would agree with me when I say how nice it is that we have the option to pass on an opportunity to be with Emma, if we have a conflict or an obligation such as a doctor visit, or if we simply feel poorly. We are capable of filling in for each other; and her parents are pretty well assured that one of us will be available when they need us. Juggling is an art we share between us; and it is working well.

I don't know your situation with your "other Grandmas", but I suggest you get together on schedules, so you can cover for each other, and give your grandchild the gift of continuity between grandparents. I'm sure the parents would be grateful. A perfect Grandma would never want to be the one to create snags in the overall scheme of things, right? Besides, if your little one is comfortable with the friendships you all share, they will tattle about things the others did, when they were there last. Don't worry, you don't ever need to repeat what they say, but it sure is fun to hear funny things they saw, or heard. You know—"Out of the mouths of babes!"

Then there are those of you who have multiple grandchildren, perhaps from different sons or daughters. Stop right here—I am either envious of you, or you have my utmost sympathy, I'm not sure which. These are unchartered waters for me. I would say that it could prove to be a real test of your juggling skills. This could get complicated. My situation is easy, my life, as I am sure you have already decided while reading this book, is simple. The idea of entertaining several children at the same time is far different that the one-on-one samples I have provided.

I concur with you. The only experience of multiple children I know is when neighbor children come to play, and I feel fairly certain that it is a poor comparison. There was no competition for Grandma's undivided attention. You, on the other hand, have very likely mastered your juggling skills, since #2 grandchild was added. You became a real expert as #'s 3 and 4 were included in the group. I give you my praise; this must have been a real challenge. With that in mind I can only hope you thought about the effects of a Grandma's bad mood or sharp tone toward any of them. A negative effect on only one, will affect another, if they are present. I certainly hope that if it is too difficult to properly care for more than one at a time that you get assistance, perhaps by Grandpa, if you have one of those. If you are doing this alone, please consider asking your sister, or a good friend, to join you for the day, or week-end, to help you, and share the joy. Think ahead, be prepared, weigh your options. There is no reason to be stressed over the time you get to spend with your grand-children. This is simply a juggling act, and you are in charge. You make the decision when to take them, so that it can be a positive experience, for everyone, every time. If you are not "up to the task" please decline. I'm sure that the parents would prefer your declination over a bad week-end for all involved. You, Grandma, are important, you're feeling count as well; and no one wants to make you feel used. That's not what being a Grandma is about.

As time progresses and you add years to not only your grandchild, or grandchildren, but your-self as well; a stay-over may be too difficult to han-dle. You may elect to limit your Grandma time to daytime only, or an occasional babysitting evening, in their home instead of yours. The parents were fully aware this day would come, and they under-stand. Their little one is no longer a toddler, but a pre-teen by now. They were raised, knowing your love for them, making it easy for you to watch over them at this time. They are simply too young to be left alone, but old enough that they do not require physical activity on your part, just your presence.

Time changes the conditions; and the juggling of school activities, social events, perhaps sports, and obviously available time, will now all fall on the shoulders of the parents. You will no longer provide the entertainment to keep your grandchild busy; they are busier than you, or their parents. You have become just one piece of the juggling puzzle being worked on. No need to worry, someone else will figure it all out. You, Grandma, can relax and let others take charge. You can agree or decline offers to "take" your grandchild, or come to their home to enjoy them as they come and go.

As long as you remain consistently kind and loving to your grandchild, you will be doing exactly as you should.

Conclusion

WHAT IS PERFECTION?

Perfection would be "Me"—or I wouldn't be writing this book.

Just kidding, perfection is perception. We are labeled and judged by every step we take. We are watched by our grandchild's parents, the nosy neighbors, our friends, and all of the other relatives.

No one agrees with everything we do; and actually very few even agree with the majority of what we do. You may appear weak in the eyes of others; and it will appear, quite often, that our grandchild is the one in charge, not us. That could be a fairly true assessment if your little one is easy to satisfy. When a child makes a request that is sweet, and simple, such as "Grandma, please play house with me", and you readily agree, it appears you are giving in to their requests in lieu of setting the plans for the day. Actually, you and your grandchild have just discovered how easy it is to enjoy a day of activities together, doing the things you have enjoyed in the past. There would be no reason to turn them down for a fun activity. The two of you have developed a nice flow that works beautifully. Hurrah for you! This is not a child who has taken charge; they are simply enjoying a good friend, called "Grandma".

Perhaps you allow a toy at the local department store, just because they asked for it. There is absolutely nothing wrong with that, as long as you know there would be no issue if you denied the request. It is your decision, and no one else plays a part, except your sweet one. Maybe the day went especially well, and they helped you clean the living room after play time, without being asked, just to surprise you. It was a positive step on their part and you are thrilled to do something special in return.

Others who judge us on our actions rarely know the full story; and besides it is not their business. We develop our own standards of what we expect from our grandchild. After all, we still adhere to the "parents rules" as we promised; and we stay "in the loop" with the other grandparents on the important issues, so what else is needed? Nobody cares what the neighbors think; and distant relatives don't count. Besides, unless they are also grandparents, they have no valid basis to provide an opinion.

Your grandchild is the only one who will decide if you are a "Perfect Grandma", or not. They will simply love you today, and for many years to come, without judgment. It is only after they are grown, and possibly after you have gone, that they will decide that you were perfect.

They will hear stories from their friends, about situations with grandparents that went poorly. Or they will hear about grandparents who were too busy to bother with them; and even grandparents who were actually mean to them. But your grandchild will only remember your efforts to make their childhood happy and wonderful. They will not be able to recall angry words or ugly glances, because there were none. Laughter and adventures will come to mind; or sweet hugs and silly stories will fill their memories of you; but nothing negative.

You are building the foundation today; and enjoying the ever-changing stages as they have grown from infancy, to toddler, and beyond. You and I are working on their happiness as we teach them all the things we have learned over our many years. We share funny tales and many sweet moments with an abundance of love in the mix.

You and I are the ones they count on to take care of boo-boo's when they are away from the comforts of Mommy and Daddy; and they know they are safe when they are with us. There are no fears, or monsters under the bed, that we cannot handle; and they trust us completely.

You can be a "Perfect Grandma" if you want to; and the only one whose opinion matters anyway, is your grandchild.

So be marvelous, be grand, and be perfect— Grandma!

Made in the USA
Charleston, SC
15 October 2013